The Jesus I Know

The Jesus I Know

HONEST CONVERSATIONS AND DIVERSE OPINIONS ABOUT **WHO HE IS**

KATHIE LEE GIFFORD

W Publishing Group

An Imprint of Thomas Nelson

Published in Nashville, Tennessee, by W Publishing Group, an imprint of Thomas Nelson.

Thomas Nelson titles may be purchased in bulk for educational, business, fund-raising, or sales promotional use. For information, please email SpecialMarkets@ThomasNelson.com.

All italics added to direct Scripture quotations reflect the author's emphasis.

Statistic used by Emilie Wierda as part of the Conclusion is taken from *Global Christianity: A Report on the Size and Distribution of the World's Christian Population* (Washington, DC: Pew Research Center, 2011), https://www.pewforum.org/2011/12/19/global-christianity-exec/.

Library of Congress Cataloging-in-Publication Data

Names: Gifford, Kathie Lee, 1953- author.
Title: The Jesus I know : honest conversations and diverse opinions about him / Kathie Lee Gifford.
Description: Nashville, Tennessee: W Publishing Group, [2021] | Includes bibliographical references.
Identifiers: LCCN 2021021570 (print) | LCCN 2021021571 (ebook) | ISBN 9780785254768 | ISBN 9780785255055 (ebook)
Subjects: LCSH: Jesus Christ. | Gifford, Kathie Lee, 1953—Religion. | Celebrities—Religious life. | Celebrities—Interviews. | Spirituality—Christianity. | BISAC: RELIGION / Christian Living / Inspirational | RELIGION / Spirituality
Classification: LCC BT304.9 .G54 2021 (print) | LCC BT304.9 (ebook) | DDC 232—dc23
LC record available at https://lccn.loc.gov/2021021570
LC ebook record available at https://lccn.loc.gov/2021021571

Printed in the United States of America

21 22 23 24 25 LSC 10 9 8 7 6 5 4 3 2 1

In a difficult year of so much loss in so many people's lives, I'm profoundly aware of the blessings I still have and even more grateful for what I have gained. Both my children married the loves of their lives in 2020: Cassidy married Ben Wierda on June 7 in Michigan, and Cody married Erika Brown on September 5 in Connecticut. My beautiful family is growing!

I dedicate this book to my four children: two of whom I carried in my womb, and the other two whom I've been praying for since they were being carried in their mothers'!

How good is our God?

Kadosh

He is in the wind
He is in the wonder
He's always been
He'll ever be
He's in the still
He's in the thunder
He's ever been, eternally
He's in the dawn of every morning
He's in the set of every sun
He's in the breath of every moment
He is Kadosh, the Holy One
Kadosh, Kadosh, Kadosh

—Kathie Lee Gifford and Richard Spitz

CONTENTS

INTRODUCTION

SURPRISING ENCOUNTERS WITH JESUS

My very first encounter with Jesus was in a dream. I was a young girl in Annapolis, Maryland, and I remember I was raking leaves with my daddy in front of our house. I looked up at the sky, and, suddenly, there I saw Him, sitting cross-legged on a cloud. I knew exactly who it was—there was no doubt in my young mind. It was Jesus.

Our eyes met, and He smiled at me and said one word. It was all my young heart needed to hear: *Kathie.*

I fell to the ground, as if dead. And yet, clearly, I was still very much alive.

Several years later, when I was twelve, my brother and I went to a small theater in our town to watch a movie by the Billy Graham Evangelistic Association. And where did God touch my heart? In a movie theater, right where I lived and breathed! I'd always wanted to be an actress and a singer and a writer, and that's exactly where Jesus met me. As I watched the movie, I heard a voice speak to me directly. Although it wasn't audible, I sensed the Lord saying in my spirit, *Kathie, I love you. If you'll trust Me, I'll make something beautiful out of your life.*

When the movie ended, they said, "If anybody wants to receive Jesus into your heart, come forward." I couldn't get out of my seat fast enough! Standing at the front of the theater, I asked Jesus into my heart. That's how my walk with Jesus began, and He has made something beautiful out of my life.

Those are just glimpses of the Jesus I know, the Jesus who has revealed Himself to me, the Jesus I am getting to know more every day. The Jesus I know is a personal God who knows me intimately but loves me passionately anyway. The Jesus I know is the epitome of grace, the radical incarnation of His Father's face and merciful eyes. The Jesus I know is the perfection of all creation.

He is love. And He loves us. Period.

In this book, you will read honest conversations about different encounters with this same Jesus. These are people God brought into my life, and they mean a great deal to me for many reasons. Some of their names will be familiar to you, and others won't. But each one has a profoundly personal and powerful story to tell about Jesus, a story that cannot be tied up neatly with a bow. Why? Because their stories aren't finished yet. Neither is mine, and neither is yours. If we are still breathing, we're not done yet; it's as simple as that!

Jesus is always the same, but He doesn't show up the same way to everyone. We are unique individuals who come from different places with different-shaped and -colored faces and different sets of circumstances. But for me, that is the eternal beauty of how our Creator seeks us and meets us right where we live and breathe, and then we begin the journey of a lifetime.

Every one of my friends' experiences with Jesus is special to me. Some of their stories will surprise you. In fact, the stories I've included in this book are just a few of the many examples of my being continually surprised by people I had no idea believed in Jesus.

For instance, years ago when I was being maliciously attacked in the media for my so-called sweatshops that didn't even exist, I got a phone call at home from Kevin Costner, whom I had met through my show with Regis Philbin. After saying hello, Kevin said to me in that familiar voice of his, "Kathie, remember, 'Greater is he that is in you, than he that is in the world.'"

I was stunned to hear him quoting 1 John 4:4. Incredulous, I asked him, "Were you raised in the church?"

He chuckled and said, "Yes, but I certainly haven't followed everything I learned." Then he went on to encourage me not to give up, not to listen to ignorant critics, and to keep holding my head up high until the storm passed because he knew it would. I deeply appreciated Kevin taking the time to find my number and then calling me to be a blessing to me. That call began a friendship that continues today.

Another time, I was interviewing the beautiful, brilliant actress Angela Bassett, who leaned over after we cut to commercial and said softly, "I'm praying for you, sister." I had no idea she was a fellow believer, and I have prayed for her ever since.

My favorite surprise came from my dear agnostic friend, Craig Ferguson. We were on the set of the film I wrote for him, *Then Came You*, and we were waiting to shoot our next scene. We were nearing the end of our six-week production and had shared many respectful, lively conversations about faith and Jesus. "You know, Kathie," Craig said in that delicious Scottish brogue of his, "I still don't believe in your guy."

"You mean, *our* guy?" I said, chuckling.

"Okay, our guy," he acknowledged.

"But I also know you believe that the way He lived his life and the way He taught us to live is exactly the way that we should."

"One hundred percent!" he exclaimed.

"Welcome to the kingdom of heaven," I said, and I hugged him. And we went back to work.

I believe with everything in me that the Holy Spirit is still working in Kevin's and Angela's and Craig's lives because God loves them and will never let them go. He will continue to pursue them, just as He continues to pursue you and me. No matter how long it takes, the Holy Spirit will finish what He starts in us. If we are faithful, we can know Him, "The God of the How and When."

I despise labels that try to define people and then relegate them to tiny boxes on a shelf. Therefore, I am vehemently opposed to the concept of "canceling" anyone or saying anyone is too far gone for Jesus to reach them. That is the complete opposite of what Jesus did two thousand years ago and what He still does on a daily basis in the lives of billions of people all over the world. I am just one of them!

Many people around us every day are encountering Jesus in their own ways. Recently, I was talking to my dear friend and former *Today* show cohost Hoda Kotb about our faith. She said, "How important is God to me? Well, I have a conversation with God just about every morning. Sometimes it's simply thank you for the two little girls sleeping upstairs or a prayer for the birth moms to let them know the girls are loved. I realize my morning journal may actually be a daily note to God, filled with thank-yous. As you have often said, it is not about religion; it is about a relationship with God. Lucky me: I found He is someone I can talk to!"

The people you meet in *The Jesus I Know: Honest Conversations and Diverse Opinions About Who He Is* are in various stages of knowing and experiencing Jesus. Many are still struggling, just as I am, to overcome weaknesses, unhealthy dependencies, bitter memories, or deep-seated disappointments. Some have suffered through trials and tribulations. Others have dreams that have not yet come true, and many of their questions remain unanswered. No matter where my friends are in their own spiritual journeys, they joined me in my favorite cozy chairs while I asked them, "What does Jesus look like to you right now?"

These are our honest conversations about how God is doing a mighty work in them, just as He continues to do in me and in you. Some of these stories are exciting, with incredible miracles! And some are messy, but God still broke through. In our conversations, I created an environment for these friends to tell me their truth. I pray that I will be a worthy messenger to share their extraordinary stories of faith.

I hope my friends will encourage you as you consider the Jesus *you* know, wherever you are on your spiritual journey. Maybe you have walked with Jesus for a long time. If so, you'll be inspired and perhaps moved to pray for these men and women. Perhaps you have friends who are curious about faith, and you're not sure how to talk to them about Jesus. I pray that my honest conversations in this book will be an example of how to interact compassionately and genuinely with people in various stages of their journeys with Jesus.

Maybe you have no idea who Jesus is, but you're interested in learning more. What an adventure you're about to begin as you read these conversations! All we have to do is welcome His Holy Spirit into our lives and then get out of His way. Moment by moment, day after day, and year after year, God sets His own pace to accomplish His purposes. Because God doesn't just show up right on time—He shows off when He gets there!

Throughout these conversations, my friends and I often share scriptures that have been meaningful to us. If you are not familiar with the Bible or want to read the verses we discussed, I've included a section in the back listing the scriptures mentioned in our conversations.

My friends, two thousand years ago, Jesus said, "I am the way and the truth and the life." Forever and always, that is who He is and who He evermore shall be. Thank you for joining me in the pursuit of the truth of Him!

Lead us, Gentle Shepherd, down these rocky paths of faith, and illuminate Your truth to us. Help us to find You in the wind of their words and in the whispers of their hearts. For if we seek You, You have promised You will be found.

ONE

A DIFFERENT KIND OF MISSIONARY

KRISTIN CHENOWETH

It is impossible to keep from smiling when I think of my talented and absolutely adorable friend Kristin Chenoweth. She is simply an irresistible human being, and I am in awe of how such a tiny person can belt out seemingly impossible high notes with so much power. She's an equally gifted actress, but it is her heart I genuinely adore the most.

Not a day goes by that someone doesn't ask me about the stunning cross I wear and where they can purchase one. I always tell them this story: When Hoda and I were interviewing Kristin on *Today*, I couldn't take my eyes off her necklace. After we wrapped, I begged her to tell me where she got it. "I designed it," she answered in her twinkle voice. "I'll give it to you." And she began to unlatch it from her neck.

"No, I could never let you do that," I said honestly, and I could tell she knew I meant it.

"Well, then, I'll send you another," she said. And true to her word, two beautiful crosses were delivered to my door: one for me and one for my daughter, Cassidy. That is Kristin to the core!

KATHIE LEE: Kristin, you know my unbridled affection for you, my amazing respect for your gifts. Where did an elf like you come from?

KRISTIN: You know, some days I wonder. I was lucky enough to be adopted. I was born in Tulsa, and my parents who raised me also live in Tulsa. Kathie, you and I talk a lot about Jesus, how God sent His Son so we can have life. And I feel like my birth mother gave me life so I can have a life. So that's the very first miracle that I ever experienced.

I grew up outside of Tulsa in a town called Broken Arrow. I'm so glad I had that upbringing. I was a kid who sang in church. I thought I'd be the next Amy Grant, Sandi Patty. I went to school, took drama, piano, and ballet. When it came time to go to college, I knew I wanted to go to Oklahoma City University because of this teacher, Florence Birdwell. She was my mentor and helped me to become the singer and artist I am today. It really all began in church.

KATHIE LEE: Were you told you were adopted, or did it come as a surprise later in your life?

KRISTIN: My mom and dad explained to me that I came to this earth in a wonderful woman's belly, and she couldn't take care of me in the way that she wanted to, and she loved me so much that she wanted to give me to someone who could do a better job. Mom and Dad said they couldn't have another baby, and they wanted to have another baby. They had the same doctor and lawyer, and those men put two and two together. My mom was to go in for a hysterectomy, and she was disappointed not to be able to have another child. The night before I was born, the doctor called my dad and said, "I've got a baby if you want her." It was 1968, so remember the time we're talking about. So they brought my mom to the hospital, and she met me. And we went home from the hospital together!

KATHIE LEE: That is so God! You were not lucky but blessed! Do you know there is not a word in the Hebrew language for *coincidence*? There is no such thing as coincidence. God is either the sovereign God, or He is not God at all. So God was weaving His tapestry among your precious parents, this beautiful biological mother who loved you enough to make sure you'd be given everything she couldn't give you herself.

KRISTIN: Thank you for reminding me. I've made so many mistakes; I'm far from perfect. When I have another Christian woman talking to me about God, it helps me so much. It's so important.

KATHIE LEE: We can't do life alone. We were never meant to. God took one of Adam's ribs to make a woman because He knew he wasn't complete. He didn't have everything he needed yet. And then He made families because we're not supposed to be alone, not supposed to face all the challenges alone. And then He gave us a church where we can love one another and leave all the judgment up to God and just be brothers and sisters.

So God didn't make you into the next Amy Grant or Sandi Patty because you are a magnificent masterpiece in your own right!

When people say to me, "You're reinventing yourself," I say, "I didn't invent myself in the first place. God made me, and He made me unique and completely different from every other human being."

So, Kristin, God chose you, like He chose me, for another world. A world that doesn't go to church, that doesn't believe the Bible could have any relevance today, that doesn't believe Jesus existed, much less was raised from the dead for our sins. That's the world we live in today. A world that cancels you if you don't believe the way everyone else does. And you came to know early on in life how special you were—made in the image of God for something much greater than your own glory. When did you know that in your young life?

KRISTIN: I have an interesting story about that. I'd become a Christian as a child. Lots of people say, "Oh, you must not have known what you were doing," but I was in the second grade, and I knew absolutely what I was doing. I mean, I just came home and told my mom, "God sent His Son to die for our sins, and I'm on that train! I want to be forgiven for my mistakes."

When I knew, though, was later. I was in middle school at a church camp. I was praying, and a youth director did an altar call, which is a call when people publicly decide to become a Christian or need extra special prayer. I kept getting a call to be a missionary, and I thought, "*I'm not really the missionary type. I like ballet. I like indoors, not bugs! But okay, God, if that's what I've got to do.*"

But . . . whoa. I was accepted to go to the Vocal Arts Academy, which is a top school. They only take five to ten kids a year. And right before the program started, I had an audition for *Animal Crackers* at Paper Mill Playhouse in New Jersey. I had a decision to make. I had what I called "impressions" from God, my inner gut. I told my mom and dad, "I'm not supposed to go to the academy; I'm supposed to go to Paper Mill to do this job." And I did.

It wasn't until a couple of years later, when I was in the trenches of Broadway and film and TV and my career took off, that I started to understand what kind of missionary God was going to have me be. I've always loved to talk about my faith. Many of my friends are not believers or have different faiths, and I say to them, "Thank you for accepting me and what I believe, because I accept you and what you believe."

We get into interesting conversations. A famous friend of mine who is not a Christian said to me, "How can you believe that this earth, the planets, were not built by the big bang?"

I said, "Okay, let me put it like this: Say I'm wrong. Who made the big bang?" People are always looking for holes in my story, and I always say, "I know who was in charge. I know it was the Almighty." I try not to go too deep because I don't want to lose people.

When I was little, I asked my mom to help me memorize Matthew 7:7: "Ask and it will be given to you; seek and you will find; knock and the door will be opened to you." So I've done a lot of that. By the way, I have made tons of mistakes. I am not perfect. I've made choices I wish I hadn't. I've lost my temper and wish I could take it back so bad. But that's why Jesus died for us. That's why I say "Please forgive me" all the time.

KATHIE LEE: A lot of people have done a lot worse than lose their temper, and Jesus is the one who forgives. He's also the one who judges, thank

God. We, the church, just do nothing but judge, judge, judge without looking in the mirror at our own selves. And why do we think that's what we're on this earth to do? Jesus said, "Love one another as I have loved you" and "Love your neighbor as you love yourself." You personify that to me, and I think that's why God entrusted you with a big voice and a big career and a big life that's only just getting started. The time that was probably the most trying for you was when you had the accident on set. Tell me about that and how it challenged the faith of your childhood.

KRISTIN: Well, I was on the set of that wonderful TV show *The Good Wife.* I had just returned from a tour in Australia, and I was on such a high in life. Unfortunately, I was outdoors in Brooklyn by the river on July 11 (I remember the date because I was going to get a free Slurpee at 7-Eleven and the date was 7/11!), and we were trying to get the last shot.

It was entirely too windy to be outside, and I heard what sounded like the flapping of a sail. They're called silks, and they're attached to almost like scaffolding beams, and they put one up about the size of ten-by-twelve. I was just waiting for "Action!" and I heard this loud noise. And I woke up in Bellevue Hospital. What had happened was, it crashed down on my head, and I crashed down on a curb. So I had a seven-inch skull fracture, concussion, tiny hairline fractures in my nose, they think cracked ribs, a bad neck, and torn disk issues. I don't remember a couple of weeks.

As I lay there, my mom and dad flew in. I had to wear a hard helmet. A lot of things changed for me in that moment. Before the accident, I wasn't the type of person to just break down. I think my body was broken. I only knew how to work, work, work. For months, I had to lay there. Plus, I had a photographic memory, and that was gone. I don't know what happened. I don't think God makes bad things happen, but sometimes I think He allows things to happen when He can't get your attention. For so long I had been going so hard and so long and never stopping, and I needed to stop and evaluate. I needed to look up, and I needed to say "Thank You," and I needed to say "I'm still now, and I can hear You." Sometimes when I get busy, it's hard for me to hear my gut, and it took me a long time to recover. In fact, I still have issues from it.

But the truth is, without that accident, I don't know that I would have come to understand when I start getting to that point again where my life is going so fast; I wouldn't recognize that moment. Also, it helped me to focus on other things, things I really want to do. Sometimes I say yes too much, and I have to get back to "I should only say yes to things I'm passionate about." The problem is that I'm passionate about a lot of things! I have to be careful because not one person can do it all.

KATHIE LEE: "Be still, and know that I am God." I think that is the scripture He has for you. What do you, my sweet friend, still long for?

KRISTIN: Joy. That's really what I am looking for. When I take a project now, I know that music is my conversation with God. I mean, I pray and read all the time, but when I sing or when I hear great music, music is my worship.

I think, for me, it's moving to Tennessee, being with someone I love greatly, hopefully making that permanent. So my next chapter is to continue to do the things I really want to do. I'm going to get to be close to okay. I've sold four projects as a producer. We know that one of those projects might make it! I'm looking forward to letting LA go and moving to Tennessee, and mainly just singing and continuing to write music, books, and just do the projects that I love to do.

TWO

FROM A JAIL CELL TO JOY

CYNTHIA GARRETT

The beautiful actress, television host, and writer Cynthia Garrett has become a close friend since I moved to Tennessee in 2018. I knew she was a powerful, dynamic woman of deep faith, but I didn't really know her story until I sat down to do this interview. I love to be surprised—and wow, did she surprise me!

Cynthia's effortless smile and effervescent personality belie the deep suffering and scars from being sexually abused as a child. I so appreciated her willingness to be vulnerable and transparent and painfully honest. My kind of woman!

KATHIE LEE: Cynthia, tell me about the family you grew up in. What did your home look like?

CYNTHIA: Well, we are six kids. You know, my mom is a good Catholic. My mom wanted six kids, and she raised us Catholic, with values and some sort of spiritual grounding. But that was really all—you know.

KATHIE LEE: Religion.

CYNTHIA: Yeah, exactly.

KATHIE LEE: You and I have grown to know the difference between religion and relationship. It is a very different thing, isn't it?

CYNTHIA: Yeah, it wasn't until I was in my late twenties that I discovered relationship.

KATHIE LEE: Okay. So what was your first impression of Jesus growing up? Do you remember your first thought about Him?

CYNTHIA: I do. He was the spirit who sat on the edge of my bed in my room at night, when I was a little girl, and comforted me when I was crying myself to sleep because I was being sexually abused by a family member.

KATHIE LEE: Wow. How old were you?

CYNTHIA: Probably from the time I was about seven to ten.

KATHIE LEE: So what was Jesus saying to you? What do you remember of Him then?

CYNTHIA: I would say to Him, "*I don't understand why this is happening to me.*" And He would say to me, "*I've got plans for you. I'm here for you, and I love you and I will get you through this.*"

KATHIE LEE: How long did the abuse go on?

CYNTHIA: For a few years.

KATHIE LEE: Okay. Then you went through a bit of a "wild girl" time. What did Jesus look like to you then?

CYNTHIA: Well, He was always my best friend and the only person I trusted.

KATHIE LEE: I've always said that anything we lose or don't receive in childhood, we spend the rest of our lives trying to get it. And almost always in the wrong ways, with destructive choices.

CYNTHIA: Oh yeah. I put walls around my heart. I would leave first. I would never allow myself to be in a position where I could be devastated.

KATHIE LEE: So you never gave your heart to anybody?

CYNTHIA: The one time I did, I got so crushed. I fell in love right after college. We called each other soul mates, he could complete my sentences, and he was bigger than life. We got engaged. And his parents started discipling me and leading me to Christ in a powerful way. They were everything I wanted to be. And they loved me.

KATHIE LEE: It was real.

CYNTHIA: It was real, oh yeah. When I went to their home, I thought, "*Oh wow, they are watching Christian TV.*" It was all about God.

KATHIE LEE: That's the beautiful thing.

CYNTHIA: So I knew He was calling me back into relationship with Him. And I thought, "*This is perfect.*" Then their son got cancer. And in his fear and insecurity, he cheated. I was devastated. He was the first person I had made myself vulnerable to.

KATHIE LEE: So deep. That's why these soul ties are so important.

CYNTHIA: Yeah. I was hurting. And at that time, Lenny was living with me in my apartment in West Hollywood.

KATHIE LEE: Tell everybody who Lenny is.

CYNTHIA: Okay, so Lenny is Lenny Kravitz. To the world, he is this handsome rock star who is insanely talented, but to me, he's been my friend since we were fifteen.

KATHIE LEE: He is your half brother?

CYNTHIA: No, we aren't related. We're just really close, and we've called each other brother and sister since we were kids.

KATHIE LEE: Okay, it's clear now.

CYNTHIA: It's funny because Lenny was the first guy who would tell me I was talented and beautiful, but I didn't need to do anything to have his admiration. So it was very healing for me. I also believed in him. Oh, the stories we have of our dreams and supporting each other! He was very much a part of my healing in my life, as a friend and as a man.

KATHIE LEE: Did you tell him everything?

CYNTHIA: Oh gosh, yeah, probably too much. With Lenny, it was totally pure; there was complete intimacy. I could cry and say, "This guy broke my heart," or I could say, "I feel ugly," and he would say, "Come on, girl, you are amazing. What are you talking about?"

KATHIE LEE: So totally safe—

CYNTHIA: Yeah, totally safe.

KATHIE LEE: That's a beautiful gift. And he had a real importance to you in turning your heart back to God?

CYNTHIA: Yeah. Lenny found the Lord at fifteen years old. So he was this kid taking the bus to South Central LA to go to Bible study. And there were times when he would look at me and the choices I was making. I was dealing with emotions that were causing me to harm myself in a lot of ways, whether it was with guys or with drugs. Lenny never judged me, but he would say things like, "Hey, easy girl," you know, like, "That guy is not worth your time," and "You need to love yourself."

KATHIE LEE: That's fascinating. What happened next?

CYNTHIA: I rebounded after that heartbreak because that relationship was my first love, where I let my walls down. And when it ended, I was in so much pain.

KATHIE LEE: It crushed you.

CYNTHIA: It crushed me. But instead of rebounding in the Lord, whom I was beginning to find at that time with my fiancé's parents, I rebounded with a very bad guy. I was in a lot of confusion and pain, and my crowd had gotten a little too into partying and drugs. I needed a way out.

So this gorgeous model guy came along. I met him at a grocery store, and he gave me his phone number. He said, "Call me if you are bored later." Later that night, I called him. I knew he was a bad guy. Everything inside me said no. Lenny met him a few times, and he said, "There is something about this guy I don't like." But to make a long story short, we were together about a month in California. Then I ran off to Europe two months later to marry him.

KATHIE LEE: You did marry him!

CYNTHIA: I ran off to Paris, got married to him. But it was total chaos with this guy, who became a completely different human being when I got there. Now I was living in "Oh no. I've brought my mom and my friends here for this wedding, and I don't know who this person is. I'm in complete pain, and I don't want to fail."

KATHIE LEE: What a nightmare.

CYNTHIA: Yeah. I got through the wedding with all those people there, and we left to go on our honeymoon in a car. And as we were racing through the South of France, I kept questioning him, "Why are you so angry?

What's going on with you?" He was using me, and I was using him as a means of escape from my life and these emotions I didn't know what to do with, which were centered in my brokenness from my childhood sexual abuse.

KATHIE LEE: That's another story.

CYNTHIA: Yeah. So I was with this guy, who was now my husband, that I really don't know. And we are racing through the night, crossing the border, going into Italy. And I discovered, while we were in the car, he was trafficking drugs. The dashboard of the car had over a kilo of cocaine in it. I ended up being arrested with him and spent three months in prison in Italy and two years testifying in trials just to get out with my life.

KATHIE LEE: Wow. What happened to your faith during that time?

CYNTHIA: In those three months, in a prison cell in Italy, I met Jesus in the most miraculous ways. I was raised a Catholic. I always knew that Jesus was real, and I talked to Him as a little girl, trying to get through what was happening to me. But then He began to appear to me in my dreams.

On my third day being locked up, I said, "God, if You are real, I need You to show me what's going to happen to me for the next twenty years of my life," because they told me I was going to be in jail for twenty years for internationally trafficking drugs with this guy.

KATHIE LEE: Oh, wow.

CYNTHIA: So on night three, I went to sleep begging God to show up. And in my dream, an angel appeared to me. It was very cinematic. I always say, "God communicates with us in the ways that we can receive," and I'm an artist—

KATHIE LEE: This is where we live.

CYNTHIA: Right. It was really real. And this angel in my dream, she looked exactly like my grandma, a full-blooded Italian with brown hair and beautiful crystal-blue eyes. The angel was dressed all in white from head to toe. She held out a book to me, and the cover of the book said "The Good News." She said, "*Do you know what the Word of God is?*" I said, "*No.*" And she said, "*Well, this is God's Word. It's your good news,* *and if you read it and commit your life to it, He will save you. And it will change your life."*

I don't know to this day if it was a vision or a dream or what it was. Theologically, I've never been able to make it make sense, but it's what I base my entire faith on because I know it was real.

KATHIE LEE: God is full of mystery.

CYNTHIA: Yes, it's how God encountered me. When I woke up, I wrote it all down. The next morning, I got a knock on my cell door. The brigadier who ran the women's side of the prison came to my door, and she brought a girl from the cell next to me, Rita, to translate.

They said to me, "There is someone coming to see you. She comes to visit the incarcerated." I thought, "*Okay.*" I heard footsteps in the stone hall. And this woman came. She was dressed in all white from head to toe, and she was a nun. She was exactly the angel from my dreams, exactly! She looked exactly like her.

She held out a book to me, and she said, "Do you know what this is? This is God's Word, and if you read it, it will change your life." On the book, it said "Good News Bible," and I fainted. When they woke me up, I cried, and I cried. At that point, I couldn't explain to them about the dream I'd had the night before. Eventually, I became fluent in Italian, and I could.

KATHIE LEE: And that dream was lived out in reality.

CYNTHIA: Yeah. It turned out that she was the head nun in the convent; we would call her the Mother Superior. We became very dear friends and are still friends to this day.

KATHIE LEE: What was her name, honey?

CYNTHIA: Well, this is the irony. Her name is Suora Angela. In Italian, *Suora* means "sister" and *Angela* means "angel." Sister Angel. Only God! She was the person the judge gave permission to drive me to my doctor's appointments. Because after about two months in prison, I started feeling sick every morning. They said, "There is no way you are pregnant. You took a pregnancy test when you were arrested." But God kept telling me through Scripture, "*I have a miracle for you, and it was* *prepared for you before you even went into this experience. You just need to trust Me."*

They eventually let me take a pregnancy test. And on Christmas morning, Suora Angela came to my cell and said, "You are pregnant." So there I was in prison with all this chaos and stress, and I was pregnant. And she said, "You need to be very calm." I hadn't spoken to my family. I didn't know if anyone knew where I was.

The consulate was finally able to get it approved so I could call my mom. She had already heard from the attorneys that I was pregnant. And my mom is a Catholic; she does not believe in abortion. But she said to me, "You do not have to keep this baby with this man if you are traumatized in any way."

And I said, "Mom, this baby is my promise from God. He is my miracle." And she said, "Great, okay." I didn't even know what I was saying, Kathie, except I knew that this child was going to be my anchor in life.

KATHIE LEE: Is that Christian, your son?

CYNTHIA: That's Christian, my son. His name is Christian Abraham, because I was praying for faith like Abraham to get through the mess I was in. And I named him Christian because I knew he was my promise from Christ. And I met Jesus in that experience in a way that I've never, ever encountered again. I got saved, and then I started working out my brokenness.

KATHIE LEE: That's right, the renewing of your heart and mind. That's where the real work begins.

CYNTHIA: Yeah, "Be ye continually renewed by Christ Jesus." And so, in my renewal, there came that day of real surrender, where I said, "God, You saved me in this epic way. You gave me this beautiful boy. I know that I've pursued my career more than You." And I got on my face; I remember the prayer. I said, "God, You can take the career, You can take the famous friends, You can take all of it. All I want is for my son to know You the way I promised You that he would know You, and I haven't done my job."

KATHIE LEE: This is biblical stuff.

CYNTHIA: Yeah. As the Scripture says, "I counted all as loss for the excellency of knowing Christ." That was really it.

After that prayer, about a month later, I was flying to Philadelphia because I had a line of jewelry on QVC. And I had my Bible on my lap. And in the aisle seat next to me, this guy said, "So. Do you read that thing?" I looked over at this guy and thought, "*Oh great, some jerk is going to tease me because I read the Bible. That's not very cool.*"

KATHIE LEE: Or sexy.

CYNTHIA: Or sexy, right. And I said, "Yeah, I do," and I brushed him off and went back to my Bible. Then he leaned over again and said, "So what are you reading?" I saw he had a wedding ring on, and I gave him a look of death.

Then this man, who introduced himself as Roger, reached in his briefcase and pulled out a Bible. He said, "I'm not hitting on you. It's just that I read it, too, and God has been speaking to me about you since this plane took off. And I've got a word for you." And he gave me a scripture. He said, "Read it. Because God loves you, and you don't look like you know that."

KATHIE LEE: Wow.

CYNTHIA: And I turned to the scripture, and I was completely convicted. I would learn that this man had an airline ministry. So if you sit next to Roger Charles at thirty thousand feet—

KATHIE LEE: You are going to come to know Jesus.

CYNTHIA: Yeah. And if you think you know Jesus, you are going to know Him deeper. I didn't realize, "This is just Roger." So I asked him, "How do I witness Christ to a Jewish person? All my friends are Jewish, and I love them so much, and I want them to know Jesus."

He said, "Okay, I will teach you how to witness Christ only out of the Old Testament. When I'm done teaching you this, you are going to be able to witness Christ to any Jew."

KATHIE LEE: Yeah. It's there. It's crystal.

CYNTHIA: Yeah, it's crystal clear. So we talked and talked. And I began this growing friendship with Roger. I assumed Roger was married, so we were just friends. He became my best friend.

KATHIE LEE: And mentor.

CYNTHIA: Yes, and mentor. One day I called him for prayer, and we prayed together. And when we got done, he said, "I need to talk to you about something." And I said, "What?" He said, "I haven't told you this, and I feel dishonest, but my wife and I are separated and divorcing." I asked, "Why do you still wear your wedding ring? You could have told me. No issues." And he said, "Because God hasn't given me release to date, and it's not right to discuss her with you."

I was like, "*What? A guy who doesn't want to throw his ex under a bus in LA?*" I had so much respect for him, Kathie. I'd never met a man with integrity like his.

KATHIE LEE: That's a real sign of integrity.

CYNTHIA: It is. Roger never talked about her badly. So after he came clean about that, the Lord spoke to me and said, "*This is your husband.*"

I thought, "*Well, I've friend-zoned him so hard. Help me to get out of this, Lord.*" I just cried, but Roger got it. He was like, "I was waiting for you to figure it out." And that's how I married my best friend.

KATHIE LEE: Wow, what a story.

CYNTHIA: A true restoration.

KATHIE LEE: And redemption! Thank you, Cynthia. It's an unbelievable story. Wow, thank you.

We get to hear Roger's story in my interview with him in chapter 19.

THREE

FAITH AS A PART OF LIFE

KRIS JENNER

By now the whole world knows about the Kardashian-Jenner family after nineteen seasons on worldwide television. They have become an international empire and continue to fascinate audiences around the globe.

But when I met Kris in the mid-1970s in California, she was a wife and a mother to two beautiful, young girls, Kourtney and Kim. Although Kris was not in show business at the time, she was surrounded by it—married to Robert Kardashian, the cofounder of *R&R* magazine, and best friends with O. J. Simpson's wife, Nicole.

Kris is also a strong believer in Jesus, and that is what bonded us together more than forty years ago. We have been through thick and thicker, and as thin as you can get, so I am so happy to share this side of Kris—the side I love the best.

KATHIE LEE: What is your earliest memory of Jesus?

KRIS: I think my earliest memory of Jesus and the Bible kind of went together for me at a very early age because my mom took us to

Sunday school when we were children. My mom told me that when I was a baby, she took me, with my grandmother, and they had me baptized. And then I started going at, like, six years old to Sunday school. And I remember my grandmother for Easter gave my sister and me little white Bibles with our names on them. I took it to my First Communion. We had a ceremony, and we stood on the front steps of the church. That memory is so vivid in my mind. And to this day, I still have that Bible.

KATHIE LEE: When you were a little girl thinking about the person of Jesus, was He real to you? What did you think about Him?

KRIS: Well, I guess I thought Jesus was just a part of my life. There was Jesus, and there was God and the Holy Spirit. I was raised with "Sundays are going to church. We're going to respect and worship the Lord God our Savior, my Savior." This is the person in my mind at six who was going to be in my life forever. I was raised, "Do unto others as you would have them do unto you." And I was also raised, "Respect the Lord Jesus Christ as your Savior. You have to have respect for the Word." I never at a young age understood what the Word was. I just knew it was a very sacred thing, and this Person was going to save me. And I signed up to be saved.

KATHIE LEE: So you had no idea at that young age how many times you'd need Him to save you?

KRIS: Oh, Lord, no. I would've been much more enthusiastic, trust me! But I was taught by the people who raised me: my mother, grandmother, father, stepfather, grandfather. My whole family. And as I grew older and met friends like you who are also believers, I took great pride in surrounding myself with people who believed the same things I believed.

I was always a good person, a good student. I was a rule follower. I believe it was the Christian background that I had. The big emphasis in those days was the Ten Commandments. My grandmother gave me, when I was about ten years old, a little charm bracelet with ten charms. Each charm was a little baby Bible and had one commandment on it. I gave it to my first two granddaughters. Now that I think of it, I should have some more made to give to the rest of them. Who knew I'd have ten grandkids! It's expensive.

KATHIE LEE: Ha ha. I think you can afford it. You're ten grandchildren ahead of me!

KRIS: All these memories sprinkled throughout my childhood meant so much. And it was always a big celebration on Easter. But it wasn't just a bunch of candy and baskets. We were taught what Easter was all about, and I was fascinated by the story that Jesus could rise again, and the rock rolled back from the tomb, and the tragedy of what Jesus went through when He was put on the cross. I guess I just always had such sympathy for that as I got older, trying to understand what it all meant. So I had this relationship that was there, and I didn't even realize it.

KATHIE LEE: Thank God for your mother and grandmother to birth that in you so early in life because you were going to really be calling on that in a few decades.

KRIS: Right.

KATHIE LEE: So as you went forward in life, you married Robert, who was quite a bit older than you. A very successful but a godly guy, wasn't he? Tell me about Robert.

KRIS: Robert was a true Christian. When I first met him, he was going to Bible study groups. So we started dating, and when we spent a little more time together, if it was Tuesday night, he would say, "Oh, I'm going to Bible study. Would you like to go with me?"

I remember the first one I attended was at Pat Boone's house. We went over there, and I thought it was fascinating to see all these people really sharing from their hearts and their love for the Lord Jesus Christ and the Word. And that's when I got my first Bible that I could actually understand. It was called *The Way*. It's so old, I try to open it very carefully. I love my old one because of all my notes. So Robert bought my first Bible, and it's signed by him, which means so much to me.

He taught me. I learned by example; I was like a sponge. I would watch him, and he would highlight everything in his Bible that was important to him and what spoke to him. I really think that what was so powerful to me was his knowledge and the way he would pray before every important meeting. I thought, "*Huh, okay, I get it.*" He was powerful and successful, and he wasn't full of himself. He was having the best life and was a very important person around town and lived in a beautiful home.

KATHIE LEE: He was a mover and shaker. Tell me what he did again?

KRIS: He was a cofounder of *R&R*, which was a big music magazine at the time. They used to have these crazy conventions, and everyone in the music business would want to go to these events. Thousands of people. It would be Dolly Parton or Steve Martin, the Blues Brothers, Boz Scaggs, performing at these events. So fun. Robert was a big publishing guy. He was impressive because he led a big life.

KATHIE LEE: And yet he took time for God. Always.

KRIS: Always. God was the most important thing. I married Robert when I was twenty-two. I had Kourtney nine months, two weeks, and two days later. He was an incredible teacher as well. He was probably the most important man in my life ever. He taught me so much about forgiveness and strength and when to flex it. And he was humble about certain things. He always said to us about giving, "The Bible says when you give, you don't need to boast about it." And decades later, we found ourselves in the throes of fame. We gave a lot, but people started saying, "You don't give anything to anybody"—you know, all the haters. Nobody thinks we give anything.

KATHIE LEE: Your Father in heaven knows what you have done. The people that matter know. But you know what's interesting to me now, Kris? It's what you guys went through with the four beautiful children you had. When I met you, your life was all about being a mother.

KRIS: I was a full-time mom. I look back now and think, "*I've had nine lives,*" truly, all these experiences I've had in my life. I've been the most blessed woman in the world. I've experienced having four small children and being able to devote myself to them and live this beautiful life and have so much that I probably wasn't deserving of. You know, I've always felt overly blessed and very appreciative and grateful for every moment. And then I had the experience of having two young kids, Kendall and Kylie, who are your goddaughters, and being equally as busy but with work at the same time. So I've been a working mom and a stay-at-home mom. They're both hard but so joyful. I feel very grateful to have experienced this journey.

KATHIE LEE: Not to be sad about it, but your marriage with Robert broke up when you had the affair. You have been very honest about it. He exercised that same forgiveness he taught you about, but for you.

KRIS: Oh yeah. I mean, he wasn't excited about it when it happened, but he knew how sorry I was about it and how I needed his forgiveness as well as the Lord's forgiveness. I needed Robert's forgiveness because he was such an important person in my life. He showed grace and mercy to me and showed me what it was like to be forgiving. He taught me how to forgive.

A couple of years after we were divorced, we became the best of friends. We'd talk on the phone numerous times a day. He'd walk in the back door and have dinner with us at my house after I was married to Bruce. It was an incredible relationship that lasted until he passed. So I feel really lucky to have had that man in my life.

KATHIE LEE: Tell me about losing him, because he was— Knowing you as long as I have, the world knows all about the Bruce stuff, but Robert was the guy.

KRIS: Yeah, Robert was so amazing. I was shocked when I learned he was sick. When he passed away, it was a huge loss. It's still a huge loss for my kids and me. We talk about him all the time. He was such a part of my kids' lives, and they just took it so hard. My son actually moved in with him about two months before Robert got sick. He moved in to get through that last year and a half of high school. And Robert Sr. really taught Rob how to study and how to focus and what the mission was. Rob wanted to get into a great college, and he wanted to go to the same college his dad went to. And the only way to do that for him was to study hard and get the right counseling. There was no better college counselor than Robert Kardashian. He was really prepping him like a college prep course. And he was helping Kourtney with her college stuff.

KATHIE LEE: She was at Arizona then, right?

KRIS: She was at SMU in Dallas for a couple of years, and then she transferred to Arizona because she wanted to be with her friends. But Robert was always great at that. He was the guy who led the way with their education. And when he got sick and passed away, that responsibility shifted, and I didn't know what the heck I was doing. I was like, "Huh, I didn't go to college. How do you get in?" But the high school Rob was going to, they were so great and helped me. But aside from the educational part of it, the kids were so in love with their daddy. It was hard for them to adjust. We all had a really hard time.

KATHIE LEE: And you called Frank, and Frank helped him get into USC.

KRIS: Yes, Uncle Frank. Since he was an alumnus at USC, we asked him to write a letter saying what a good kid Rob was.

KATHIE LEE: That's the history of us, Kris. We go so far back with so many things. I don't want to make you sad about it, but in this book, I wanted people to learn something they've never known about you, that ancient part that we share.

KRIS: As a mom, at that point I was the only biological parent they had that they could count on, and the responsibility was just mine. And I just did my best. So when you guys helped me out, and other friends would step in to say, "Maybe we'll talk to the kids about this or that," it really helped. It does take a village.

KATHIE LEE: Yeah, it does! Through the years, then, I know you taught your kids about Jesus. You and Bruce even started a church in the Hidden Hills area. There was a time when you thought that was an important part of your walk.

Once the whole Kardashian thing started happening, how present was Jesus still in your life during that period? Remember, when you started doing that, I said, "Kris, they have to see how much your faith is a part of your life. The world doesn't want to hear that kind of stuff." Tell me about that time and how you kept God in your life.

KRIS: It wasn't about me trying to keep God in my life. He wasn't going to let me forget any part about Him. No matter what I did, I felt like He was talking to me. There's a verse in the Bible that goes something like, once you know the Word of God and you turn away from it, it's worse than if you never knew.

KATHIE LEE: That's right. Basically, woe to those who know the truth. So you thought that was a danger.

KRIS: That was a danger because I've always been taught about the fear of God. And I did realize that if I got too busy, then there's that saying also that "If God doesn't get you bad, He'll get you busy." So "busy" was my middle name. And I was so incredibly busy when we started the show. But right in the beginning, we had moved to this new house on Eldorado Meadow, the one with the black-and-white-checked floors. I'd get on the treadmill at 5:00 a.m. and start working out, and I'd say my prayers.

KATHIE LEE: Let's come to the present now. Give me a picture of this Jesus you met at six years old. What does He look like to you now?

KRIS: I think He's just a constant in my life. It's believing and receiving His forgiveness, receiving His love and allowing me to then be loving to other people. So many people tell me that I'm a very forgiving person. Things happen, and we have tough skin in the public eye, even personally with relationships—it's taught me to be softer, to be more forgiving and more giving.

I am put here, and my relationship with other people is important to me, but there are also sometimes people I can really help, whether it's spiritually, physically, financially. There's stuff I get to do where I realize that God is always at work in my life. And I think my children feel the same way. Kourtney and Kendall and the others, they go to Bible study once or twice a week. We had a Bible study over at Kourtney's house the other day with Jason Kennedy.

KATHIE LEE: Is there anything else you want to share? If you were to describe Jesus today, what would you say about Him?

KRIS: I think it's simply I just believe that I receive the knowledge and the power and the love, and I think He is an important part of my life and my Savior. I accept Him as that, and I have faith. And faith is such an important thing that I was taught, and now it's just a part of who I am. So it's hard to explain. It's that other important relationship in my life that I truly have faith in and believe. And I believe I can come to Jesus with my gratitude, my fears, my prayers, and the faith that I have that He can answer prayer—and the protection.

I pray every single day just to protect and keep the health of my family because that's all we have: our health and our family. I really believe that God has given us this position in life because "to whom much is given, much is required." And I believe that it may not be today or tomorrow; it may just be ongoing, like a river that keeps flowing. I really believe that when all eyes are on us, which they are daily, that we have a big voice. And I pray every day that God gives me the right message, what He wants me to say on His behalf, that what comes out of my mouth that somebody else is blessed or helped by something we can say or do for them.

FOUR

GROWING TOGETHER IN JESUS

JASON KENNEDY AND LAUREN SCRUGGS

I have been friends with Jason Kennedy since he first came on the national scene as a correspondent for *E! News*. I've always admired his natural charm, his commitment to excellence, and his public acknowledgment of his faith in Jesus.

My daughter, Cassidy, and I were honored to be guests at the ceremony when Jason married his beautiful bride, Lauren Scruggs, in Dallas, Texas, where Lauren had grown up. Lauren became known nationally when she lost her left eye and her left arm in a tragic propeller accident in 2011. She wrote a powerful book, *Still Lolo: A Spinning Propeller, a Horrific Accident, and a Family's Journey of Hope*, about the life-changing incident and her long and painful recovery.

KATHIE LEE: You guys have separate faith journeys, and now you're one in Christ and one in the flesh as a married couple. Jason, why don't you tell me the faith background you came from? Were you raised in a Christian family?

JASON: I was raised in a Southern Baptist church in South Florida. Probably until I was about fourteen or fifteen years old, I would fall asleep during the sermon. My sister would be like, "You're in middle school, and you're sleeping like a baby through the message!" I just never really connected with what was happening. But I loved Sunday school because I got to see my friends, and we got to hang out. So I would go to the Baptist church for Sunday school, and then when it was big service, I would go to the Presbyterian church to do Sunday school there because I had another set of friends. I was just a big Sunday school guy.

KATHIE LEE: You know what that translates as: "nerd."

JASON: I could do the books of the Bible in under twelve seconds. I was a really smart kid. My senior year of high school, I met one of my best friends still to this day, Rich Wilkerson Jr. His parents had an Assemblies of God church, and it was the most incredible thing ever, so I started going to church with him. That's when it really connected. As I got older and understood that Jesus not only loves you but has grace for you and forgives you and is on your side, He's for you, I think it kind of changed everything. And then when I moved to LA and was on my own, making new friends, I had that decision: "Am I gonna just do what my parents taught me, or am I gonna understand what this faith thing means for myself?" And that's when I realized I can't live without it.

KATHIE LEE: Lo, tell me a little about you growing up in Dallas, Texas.

LAUREN: My parents divorced when I was four. After that was when my parents became really serious about their faith. I went to two separate churches, my mom's and my dad's. My mom became a believer right after the divorce. And I remember every morning, she'd be in her big, cozy chair with her coffee and her blanket and her Bible and her pen. That was such an example to me, and I started to journal because I wanted to be like my mom. That kind of developed my prayer life and how to talk to God. I learned so much from my mom that way. She was so passionate about the Lord. My sister and I came to know Jesus around the same time, at about age six. We had a little Bible study with our girlfriends that my mom would lead at our house. I would go to church also with my dad on the weekends.

KATHIE LEE: What denominations were they?

LAUREN: My mom went to a nondenominational church, and my dad went to a Presbyterian church. The youth group there was one of the most amazing communities I've ever experienced. There was just so much love in that group and grace and lack of judgment and amazing teaching about the Lord. I learned so much about the importance of community there. I had so much discipleship around me, good friends, families. I got filled with a lot of the presence of the Lord.

My parents got remarried when we were around eleven years old, and they had so many couples coming over to share their own stories. I learned so much by listening to their stories of redemption, dependence on the Lord; so many different aspects really developed my faith.

Then I moved to New York my sophomore year of college, and it became truly my own faith. It was like I was developing growing up, but when I was by myself away from my family and friends, it became even more real to me in that city.

KATHIE LEE: So it's a similar story to Jason's. Getting away from everything you knew was going to be a challenge: "Am I now going to follow it or go my own way?" Did either one of you get off your path when you got immersed in the LA or New York culture?

JASON: I wouldn't say I ever considered abandoning my faith, but I definitely had fun in LA the first year. And it was probably the loneliest year of my life because I left my friends and my family. I was working at the mall and thinking I'd be on TV immediately, and it wasn't like that at all.

KATHIE LEE: What did you do at the mall?

JASON: I worked at Diesel folding jeans. My manager would yell at me because back then crinkled shirts were really in, and I'd spray the shirts and rough them up, but I wasn't roughing them up enough. And the whole time I was thinking, "*All right, God, You've got this plan and I'm* *waiting.*" The big break was *E!* I had auditioned for them on my lunch break. Six months passed. I was in Shreveport, Louisiana, visiting a friend who happened to be a pastor. He told me, "It's not going to be *if*; it's going to be *when.*" I got a call that next day saying, "We want to bring you in." And the rest was a great experience, sixteen years that I just wrapped up.

KATHIE LEE: And how do you feel about that?

JASON: I went through a mourning process for sure. I kept thinking about all the great memories, and it made me sad. And then I realized I had to surrender to the fact that God had closed that door. It was sixteen incredible years. What a long, amazing ride! And now I'm so excited, I've already had great calls and meetings, multiple new projects, and I feel so good and ready for the next season and what that looks like. I'm so grateful that you held my hand through many of those years and encouraged me.

KATHIE LEE: And I want to include the love story of the two of you.

JASON: I saw Lauren on *Dateline NBC.* She lost her arm and her eye and had a traumatic brain injury. And I just couldn't stop thinking about that story. A year after it happened, she did a handful of interviews, and I said to myself, "*Man, I would love to meet a girl like that. She just seems incredible.*" Fast-forward to a couple of months after that, she got an interview with Giuliana at *E!* Giuliana brought her to the studio, we went on a hike the next day, we communicated every single day since that time, and now we've been married for over six years.

KATHIE LEE: I can't believe it's been six years!

JASON: Yeah, I know. That was a fun wedding!

KATHIE LEE: Lo, could you talk about that season of suffering for you? Tell me about the accident in the briefest of terms, so people know the extent of your injuries.

LAUREN: I was in a little two-seater plane. Our friends live along a runway, and every home has a hangar. So I went on one of those planes to look at Christmas lights. I was on the plane, and I just knew, this whole different feeling I felt before, like something was about to happen. I prayed to the Lord, and I was like, "*I trust You with my life.*" We landed, and I still felt no relief.

KATHIE LEE: A foreboding feeling?

LAUREN: Yes, I was very adventurous, so I flew a few times with my friends and had the time of my life. But I was very fearful this time. I got out of the plane how I always had. The plane was still on, and I was hit by the plane propeller. I lost my left hand, left eye. There were way more injuries than I was aware of at the time. Crazy things, like a spinal injury, neck injury, jaw fracture, brain aneurysm—just so many things. God is so big. I literally cannot believe I'm here, functioning, able to do life. Just so wild.

I remember waking up in the hospital. I was there three weeks. I lived with my parents through the physical recovery, around six months. I was definitely going through the grieving process. I remember my doctor asked me, "Have you gotten angry yet?" I was like, "Yes." And she said, "Great!"

KATHIE LEE: What did your anger look like? Was it at God or the person who had the propeller running?

LAUREN: Actually, neither. I saw God more clearly through the accident than probably any other time in my life. I never felt anger toward God, never like, "Why me?" Definitely not toward the pilot, because I couldn't imagine what he was going through. I didn't feel anger toward them, more the anger over missing my eye and my arm. They say that losing a limb is very similar to the mourning of losing a sibling.

KATHIE LEE: Did you have concerns at that time? Were you working as a model?

LAUREN: I was reporting for fashion week but not modeling. I was working in retail while working on my magazine that had launched three months before my accident. It was exploding, and people were loving it. Looking back, I see so much of the purpose in that.

KATHIE LEE: During the time after your accident, did you ever worry that you'd never meet the man of your dreams? What were your feelings about that as a woman?

LAUREN: I feel like when you have a physical trauma, you see all your idolatry right away. I was like, "*Oh wow, I didn't realize how much I valued compliments about how I look and physical beauty. And now I don't have my hand, my eye is gone, and people are going to treat me differently. Guys are going to look at me different.*" I was grieving that, but there's such a big realization now, that is not where identity lies. What a blessing. I've talked about this with my girlfriends who have lost limbs. It immediately filters out the guys who aren't pure at heart.

KATHIE LEE: It gets rid of a lot of frogs before you have to kiss them!

LAUREN: Yes! That was a blessing. But you can't rush the healing process. In those moments, I was so blessed with the most incredible community all around me. I still would process the loss and had to depend on the Lord and go to Him in those moments. Even with all these people and so much love, I still needed something bigger. So in those moments I would go to the Lord.

KATHIE LEE: So instead of being bitter toward the Lord, it brought you much closer. Were you familiar with Jason from TV before you met him?

LAUREN: I think so. I watched *E!*, but I'm terrible with names. I'm sure I knew who he was, but I didn't know his name. I remember coming to LA, where I met Jason. There was no pressure. It was just meeting someone new and going on a hike.

KATHIE LEE: Tell me about the hike.

LAUREN: I'd met Jason on a Friday, and he asked me to text in the morning to go on a hike. So I texted him, and he gave me his address. I remember little things like he brought water bottles, and we talked about some topic, and I was like, "Oh wow, he really does know Jesus."

KATHIE LEE: You already had a crush on her, right?

JASON: Absolutely! Lo and I texted and kept in touch, and I told her I wasn't going to get serious with anybody at that time because I was doing the *Today* show a lot, flying to New York every two weeks, and the news in LA, and the idea of cross-country job stuff seemed like a lot. But it just felt right. I wanted to get to know her more, so I made frequent trips to Dallas, brought her to LA a bunch of times, and thank God it worked!

KATHIE LEE: So how long was it before you realized you were truly in love, and who knew first?

JASON: We had great moments, but for me, I think I knew it on a trip to Dallas about a year later. I was thinking, "*Maybe she should move to LA, and we'll see how it goes.*" But then I was like, "*No, I want to propose and let her know how serious I am. I can't imagine being with anyone else.*"

LAUREN: I remember a time when I was staying downstairs at his house, and I was struggling this particular day with my arm. He came home, and I told him that I'd been having a tough day. He was so sweet. He said, "I love your hand, I love your eye, and I love you."

KATHIE LEE: Now you're in a different kind of a hike: an uphill struggle to have a child. Tell me how you're feeling about it.

LAUREN: We've been trying for four years. We went to one doctor and started IUIs, but it didn't work. We have so much trust and hope in God's journey that we don't worry about it, though. We're excited about what God's timing is. We're very content in our lives and enjoy each other, and a child will only add more joy.

KATHIE LEE: Praise God. You're not letting the longing for something spoil what you already have.

LAUREN: I feel like we've been so parallel in our perspective on that.

KATHIE LEE: What would you say to other young people about love? What does love look like to you guys?

LAUREN: The first thing that comes to me is serving each other, looking above our own ways, caring about the other over ourselves. Also just having fun. Being aware emotionally of each other. Being vocal about our needs, our lives. Praying.

JASON: I never really experienced one true love before her. If there were stages to it, it was like, "Wow, this is someone who's incredible," then "She's my best friend," then "I can't imagine not having her in my life." We just have the best time together. Even through the arguments we become closer. It strengthens our relationship, and we become closer to the Lord. There are so many things that happen through trials in your relationship. I feel like we're still growing in love with each other.

It's the greatest feeling when you're not having to do the challenges that come with life alone. You have someone on your team.

KATHIE LEE: I know how much you love Lauren and that you would do anything for her.

LAUREN: Even after we got married, there's emotional healing still taking place.

JASON: Yes, and counseling has been a game changer for us. I'd never done that before. It's awesome. It's also made me want to talk to my close guy friends about our marriage. When you've got four guys, there's a good chance one or two are gonna be going through some kind of struggle, so the other two are great at reminding you, "Your wife's a queen; she's incredible." And then going home, you see it all in a better perspective.

I was going to church for me, but then I was like, "*What can I bring to the church and how can I add value to the community?*" I met Judah Smith, and he wanted to come down and do a monthly Bible study. It was ten people in my living room, and then twenty, and then a hundred people, so we moved to a hotel ballroom and then moved to another hotel ballroom and then finally to the Saban Theatre. It turned into Churchome, and during COVID it's taken on a whole new meaning. "Wait, church from home—you can have community and watch from home?" The goal wasn't to create a church but many lifelong friendships that add value to your marriage.

LAUREN: His leadership at the church and with his community of friends is just amazing.

JASON: I used to wake up and pray because I thought God would be angry with me. Now I pray all throughout the day, when I'm happy, sad, frustrated, joyful. I can't even imagine life without prayer. I can't.

KATHIE LEE: It's in Thessalonians: "Pray without ceasing." How do we do that? You make your life a prayer. "In Him we live and move and have our being." That means every nanosecond of our lives. You guys truly epitomize that. Your story is a timeless, classic love story.

FIVE

DO NOT GROW WEARY IN WELL DOING

CHYNNA PHILLIPS BALDWIN

I loved listening to the Mamas and the Papas in the 1960s. They were hip and California cool, and their beats and harmonies were magic. I dreamed of one day making a life for myself in the entertainment industry that beckoned to me from sunny California.

Chynna Phillips grew up in this world, the beautiful daughter of John and Michelle Phillips, founding members of the band. They were rock-'n'-roll royalty. And although she inherited her mother's beauty and her parents' musical talent, Chynna also fell into a life of drugs, alcohol, and abuse. Then, in 1995, she doubled the drama by marrying Billy Baldwin, one of the four famous acting Baldwin brothers.

While I'd interviewed Chynna in the past, I had never really had a conversation beyond her career with the music group Wilson Phillips, which she founded with Wendy and Carnie Wilson, daughters of rock-'n'-roll legend Brian Wilson of the Beach Boys. To say Chynna surprised me is an understatement. I found her to be raw and authentic and articulate and refreshingly brave about her life in a world very few of us could ever imagine experiencing. I fell in love with her. I think you will too.

KATHIE LEE: I was a huge fan of Wilson Phillips. I think we met when I was on with Regis.

CHYNNA: It was a crazy time. That was thirty-three years ago!

KATHIE LEE: I have to tell you, first of all, how impressed I am. I knew you were happily married, but I didn't know about your amazing YouTube channel, California Preachin'. I am so blown away by it. You come off so real and honest, and God is obviously blessing it. A lot of people have heard the headlines about your family, but what I think surprised me the most is how deep your walk with Jesus is. This is not surface Christianity.

CHYNNA: It started out much more produced: hair, makeup, teleprompter. I started getting this horrible back pain before I started to shoot. I prayed, "God, I know for sure You told me that You wanted me to do a YouTube channel, so why does it hurt?" I just got this really strong message of "*Just turn the camera on and show the world who you are. Just be you. You're not a pastor or a preacher; you're just a sheep. Go out there and be a sheep among many, and people will identify with you.*"

KATHIE LEE: You're an adorable sheep! I thought you were charming, but then I started getting really pulled in when you stripped it down raw. And made your suffering not as a victim. You're somehow doing the impossible, which is telling all these incredible things that happened in your life without begging for our compassion because you've been so victimized. You come off like, "Yeah, but God saw something in me."

This book I'm writing is *The Jesus I Know* because Jesus is so many different things to different people. It doesn't look the same ever. Because we don't look the same to Jesus. No story is like anyone else's. God went to so much trouble to make us unique. Tell me your story.

You grew up in a Hollywood family, and so did your husband. All sorts of drama. What was your picture of God when you were growing up?

CHYNNA: I had a nanny when I was one year old. Her name was Rosa Garcia, and she didn't speak a word of English. My mom grew up in Mexico City and spoke fluent Spanish, so she was ecstatic that I would have no other choice but to learn Spanish. I was basically raised by this woman. She lived with us until I was nineteen years old. She walked me to school, fed me, read my bedtime stories, danced with me, sang with me, prayed for me. I remember she had crucifixes hanging over her bed, and she had candles with Mother Mary; she was incredibly Catholic. When I was sick, she'd douse me with holy water. So that was my first introduction to Jesus.

Then when I was in a public elementary school, I was struggling. I begged to leave because I was being bullied, and my mother reluctantly transferred me to a Christian private school. She said, "You do realize they're going to talk to you about the devil and 666." But I was so miserable, I just wanted out.

About a week in at the Christian school, I stole a chocolate milk from the cafeteria. The next day, these girls came up to me and said, "Chynna, we saw that you stole the chocolate milk," and I said, "Well, I didn't have any money." I gave them a quarter, and they said, "We don't want the quarter." They said they were wondering if I'd accept Jesus as my Lord and Savior. And I thought, "*Ugh, I stole the milk; look what I've gotten myself into. Now I'm gonna have to accept Jesus Christ as my Lord and Savior. All right, fine, I'll do it.*" So they brought me to the girls' bathroom, and they all surrounded me—not awkward at all! They stood around me, and I said the words out loud on the card that they gave me. As I began to read the words, I started to feel a holy scan begin from the top of my skull, moving down my face, down my shoulders. As it was happening, I felt as though I was being completely purified. By the time it got down to my feet, I felt like I'd become a new creation. I was saying the words sincerely, but I didn't think anything would happen! I couldn't speak; I was paralyzed. I was holding on to this card, and I was thinking, "*This Jesus person is for real. This is not a joke; He's really the Son of God.*" I left the bathroom a completely changed person. He put a new heart inside of my body and made me a new creation.

I went home to the marijuana roaches in the ashtray, no Bibles in the house, no father to talk to, and a very busy single mother. I didn't know how to explain what had happened to me. I told nobody about my spiritual experience. So, basically, I stole a chocolate milk, and I got saved. A true sinner saved by grace.

And then I got into drugs and alcohol and got promiscuous. I was a Hollywood statistic kid. I was drinking, partying, hanging out with people who were just like me, until I had a second coming when I was about thirty-four years old. My husband's brother, Stephen, got saved. He's a great guy. Every time I'd see Stephen and his wife, Kennya, they'd be tagging along with their Bibles. I thought, "*Wow, they've really taken it to the next level.*"

Then about two years later, I was living in Bedford, New York. It was Super Bowl Sunday, and everybody came over. Some of my nieces got in trouble, so Stephen and his wife were praying over them with zeal. This was not just any kind of prayer. They had their hands over them, and I could hear it from the other room. The Holy Spirit said to me, "*You go in there, and you tell them, 'Whatever you're doing to them, I want you to do to me.'*" I was like, "*Oh no, here we go again.*" So I did. They said, "Are you sure you want us to pray for you?" and I said, "Yes." It happened all over again with the holy scan down my body. I was bawling.

The first thing I did was go straight to my front door. I had purchased this expensive wooden Buddha that had sat there for years. I grabbed it and wrapped it up with duct tape and put it in my garage. I said, "That's it, Jesus Christ is Lord and Savior, and I will dedicate the rest of my life to serving Him and furthering His kingdom. I'm sold out for Jesus."

KATHIE LEE: What was your husband's, Billy's, reaction?

CHYNNA: Billy was supportive, but it scared him a little bit. I mean, how do you compete with Jesus? And he knew it was a profound experience. I had an anointing. He knew something had shifted, and it was out of his control. When I was baptized a few days later, Billy cried; he was really taken by it. He went to church with me that Sunday. I figured he was going to be right behind me. I thought, "*It will just be a couple of weeks or months, and we'll raise our kids Christian,*" but that wasn't the case. He's still not completely on board, and it's been fifteen years. We do attend church together as a family, and Billy does pray with me.

KATHIE LEE: Well, He's The God of the How and When. We stand on God's promises, but only He knows how and only He knows when. And that's the maddening part, when we have to "live by faith, not by sight," because everything we're seeing is saying, "No, this is impossible." The father of lies wants to tell us deception, deceit, and discouragement—all the Ds, instead of the Rs: refresh, resurrect, renew, restore. I knew some of your story, but wow.

CHYNNA: Billy and I are polar opposites. He's into wrestling, politics, but I'm not a person who turns on CNN and reads the paper; it's just not my thing. We also struggled in our marriage. We had financial troubles, and then our son got sick. I filed for divorce at one point. There are days when I wake up, and I'm like, "Why did I do this?" But you know what? I think that's okay. Sometimes I wake up, and I go, "Ew. What have I done? I don't want to look at your face." People want the truth about the struggle and how to get through it, how to embrace the suck of your marriage.

Divorce isn't an option for me anymore. Every single day, I wake up and ask God to help me navigate my marriage. Because it's not a walk in the park. I have great days with Billy where we laugh and we're best friends; we're truly connected. No one makes me laugh like him; nobody's taught me more than him. I've never met anyone more intelligent. I know he still gets excited when he sees me singing and writing songs; he happens to think I'm very unique and special. So there's lots of wonderful things about our marriage, but we don't stroll through our marriage. We have to work at it.

KATHIE LEE: This is just fascinating. I'm listening to your story, and I'm thinking this is cool, real stuff. I loved Frank Gifford so much; he was the love of my life, and he ripped my heart out when he cheated on me. I forgave him right away because God showed me all the things He forgave me for. I got angry with Frank because it was so easy for me to forgive him that he just thought it would go right back to being the way it used to be. I went to a counselor who said, "If you can't forgive your husband, forgive your children's father." It took my eyes off of me and put them on what I needed to be concentrating on, my family. When I changed my focus, that's when my heart was softened enough to do the right thing, and God could heal. I felt love, and he felt forgiven. Only God can do that.

CHYNNA: Yes, only God. We're just not capable to forgive on that level. That's provision by God.

KATHIE LEE: He died on the cross, which is the free gift of grace. He forgives our sins daily. It's not a onetime gift; it's a gift for eternity. Forgiveness is a reliable, renewable resource that we can count on, and boy, do we need it!

CHYNNA: It's like the old adage that resentment is like drinking poison and waiting for the other person to die.

KATHIE LEE: Once you had that second born-again experience, it took root this time. How did you change? Did you become a churchgoing person?

CHYNNA: I started going to church in LA. Then we moved to Santa Barbara, and we attended a church pretty regularly, but with COVID it's almost impossible. I know that the church is the body of Christ, and I know that I need to find a home church.

KATHIE LEE: You need to find a community of believers, not necessarily a building. How are your children doing spiritually?

CHYNNA: I beat myself up because I'm like, "My children aren't reading the Bible." They believe in God. My youngest daughter, Brooke, was baptized alongside Billy's mother, Carol, several years ago. My older two were baptized by me during COVID lockdown, in my bathtub! I was hoping they'd have the holy body-scan experience, but it didn't happen that way. I cover them every morning in prayer. We used to dress our kids as babies, so why can't we dress them in prayer? I cover them in the armor of God, the shield of faith, every single day. I believe God is faithful and in God's time.

KATHIE LEE: What about when you went through your son's cancer? Were you ever angry at God?

CHYNNA: No, I wasn't angry at God. I actually thought, "*Maybe this will bring Billy to Jesus.*" Unfortunately, that wasn't God's plan. I don't know what it will take. Our son's doing great now. He just had another surgery three months ago. Because it was stage 4 cancer, he had some more tumors in his stomach, but they were not malignant, which was so huge. I truly believe that the Lord will give Vance an opportunity to share his cancer testimony with many. I have called him "war horse" as a term of endearment for many years. I never really understood why . . . but now I know.

KATHIE LEE: During that time, you still did one of your YouTube talks, but you were losing it.

CHYNNA: I didn't want to cross any boundaries with my son, and he wasn't ready for the world to know he had this surgery, so I had to talk around it. All people saw was me in this furry hat in the bathroom. Billy joked that it looked like I'd been committed. I get that it totally looked that way! It was a tough time. All the viewers supported me through it, and then I was finally able to share. My son did twenty-eight rounds of chemo. He had four different types of cancer. This one particular form of cancer was resistant to chemo, so he had to have a major surgery to remove the nonmalignant tumors.

KATHIE LEE: What would you say is the hardest thing you have to deal with on a regular basis?

CHYNNA: I still struggle with a lot of anxiety, and that's closely related to depression. I have a counselor who keeps telling me, "We're going to land your plane, Chynna. There's going to be a lot of turbulence, the descent is not going to be easy, but we're going to land it." I'm having faith that my plane's going to land.

I have a lot of PTSD—not only did my son have cancer, but we had a mudslide and lost twenty-eight people in our community. And then my "other mother" passed away. We all called her Granny Jax. She witnessed all three of my children being born. I love my mother with all my heart, but this woman showed up for me in a way that my mom could not, and I lost her too. This all happened back-to-back.

I have this issue of not feeling like God loves me or that God's there for me. I believe in God and that He's real and that Jesus is His Son, but I have such deep-seated abandonment issues that for years I couldn't call God "Father." I felt no connection to that word, and now just recently I've been able to call God "Father" organically, and I actually feel the connection when I say it. It's been a long fifteen years of not feeling that God loves me and is present in my life. I know I'm not alone in this.

KATHIE LEE: Basically, your story is that the struggle goes on. Do you ever want to give up? Say, "Okay, Jesus, I love You, but this isn't working for me"?

CHYNNA: I'll say six months ago was the lowest I've been, when Vance had to go back in for surgery. I thought, "*I don't know what You think I'm made of, but I can't do this anymore. You're going to have to pick someone else.*" I didn't have one more ounce to keep fighting, but I thought, "*If my son is still fighting, then I have to also.*"

I begged them during COVID to let me be by Vance's side in the hospital. I'd already had COVID and had the antibodies, so they let me stay. I slept on a cot in his room for ten days. We bonded, we laughed, we cried. It was extraordinary. And then I couldn't get out of bed for like two weeks, I was so spent. After ten days of just focusing on what needed to get done for our child, the emotional aspect was just so draining. I was weary.

KATHIE LEE: The Lord says, "Do not grow weary in well doing," because He knew we would get weary in well doing. He says, "*You don't have to; I am enough. I've carried it all before, and I can carry it again for you.*" I love your story because it doesn't have a beginning, a middle, and an end. It's ongoing. Thank you for sharing it.

SIX

A DOUBLE PORTION OF SHAME, A DOUBLE PORTION OF BLESSING

ANNE FERRELL TATA

Many of you know of my deep friendship with the brilliant artist Anne Neilson, admired internationally for her beautiful *Angel* paintings. Years ago Anne introduced me to one of her favorite friends, Anne Ferrell Tata, a Southern girl with a Southern double name, and she quickly turned into one of my dearest friends as well.

You simply can't resist Anne Ferrell's infectious, wide-eyed wonder at life and her joyful, ever-optimistic embrace of all things the Scripture calls "praiseworthy." Anne Ferrell has a deep commitment to studying the Word of God, and she is one of my most faithful prayer partners.

Anne Ferrell reminds me of Gidget—remember her? Anne Ferrell is just adorable. But who could have known that she carried an anything-but-innocent secret inside her for three years? We sat down recently to talk about that dark season of her life.

KATHIE LEE: Anne Ferrell, did you grow up in a godly home?

ANNE FERRELL: Absolutely, yes. My dad was a minister, and my mom has a master's in Christian education.

KATHIE LEE: Tell me your story, honey. Obviously, you grew up with a knowledge and a love for the Lord Jesus, didn't you?

ANNE FERRELL: Yes, He was my Lord and Savior. I didn't have a moment when I said, "Lord, I accept You as my Lord and Savior." I felt like I always knew Him. We grew up saying grace and night prayers and reading Scripture. Jesus was very much a part of our family.

KATHIE LEE: So you had a great life, and then you met your future husband, Bob. When was that?

ANNE FERRELL: I had just graduated from college. Bob was my first real boyfriend. I remember our first date, because I was very honest with him. You know how usually on a first date you're trying to be impressive, right?

KATHIE LEE: Right, yep.

ANNE FERRELL: I thought, "*I don't care. I'm never going to see this guy again.*" So I was blunt with him. I told Bob on our first date, "I believe God has only one man for me, and one day I will know who that is." I also told him I'd have four children, including one named Peyton and one named Preston, and I would not marry Catholic.

KATHIE LEE: Was he Catholic?

ANNE FERRELL: Yes.

KATHIE LEE: Wow!

ANNE FERRELL: He says he was like, "Challenge accepted. I'll get this girl to marry me."

KATHIE LEE: So then what happened?

ANNE FERRELL: Bob quickly became my favorite date. He's just one of the funniest guys. It was so fun, and it was no pressure because he very much respected me and let me guide the timing of everything.

KATHIE LEE: Oh, so you had fun.

ANNE FERRELL: Yeah. He was in the US Navy at the time, and he had to go away for two weeks. The day he left, it hit me so hard. I was like, "*Oh, my gosh, I didn't see this coming—but I'm in love with him.*"

KATHIE LEE: Yep.

ANNE FERRELL: I was like, "*Why didn't I try to be more impressive?*" I was beating myself up because I thought I had blown it. Then I got a card from him in the mail. I thought, "*Okay, he still likes me.*"

KATHIE LEE: You wanted to make yourself irresistible this time.

ANNE FERRELL: Exactly.

KATHIE LEE: So he came back from the two weeks, and what happened?

ANNE FERRELL: He came back, and it was clear that we really missed each other. We did a lot of stuff together. Then about a month later, he told me he loved me, and I said, "I love you." And he asked me to come to Virginia with him to meet his family. That's when I knew we were probably going to get married.

KATHIE LEE: And how old were you, sweetie?

ANNE FERRELL: I was twenty-two. He was twenty-six.

KATHIE LEE: So you got married?

ANNE FERRELL: Yes. We had such a fast romance. I called my friends to say, "I'm getting married!" and they were like, "Who are you dating?" So Bob and I got married, and we moved to Virginia. The first five years of our marriage, we had a blast because he was my best friend. Everything was great. Then his third year at law school, one day we were just like, "Let's have a baby." And I had two kids within two years. Then all hell broke loose.

KATHIE LEE: All right, tell me what happened.

ANNE FERRELL: I really want to honor Bob in telling this. We both were working full-time. We had been married about eight years, with two small children. He was climbing the ladder of his law firm. And he was ambitious, which, of course, is one of the things I loved about him. I worked out of our home and took care of the kids. On the outside it looked like, "Wow, they have it all," but on the inside I was dying. I was lonely, I was depressed, and I felt empty.

KATHIE LEE: Why?

ANNE FERRELL: I was exhausted. Plus, I tried to keep it all in. I'm from the South, where you don't air your dirty laundry. And I was so busy, I didn't have time to deal with it. I just kept going. Again, I'm not blaming Bob in any way. We were moving fast paced.

KATHIE LEE: Do you think you were taking each other for granted?

ANNE FERRELL: Yeah. I kept saying, "We need counseling." He was like, "I'm fine." So I started going to a counselor by myself. I went for several months, and I realized a lot of things.

At the time, my best friend was working as a model in New York City. One day I told Bob, "I want to go see Diane," and I just took off to see my friend. She's absolutely stunning. Everywhere we went in the city, though, I got all the attention. It was the craziest thing. And you know what? I've thought since then, men can detect a woman in distress. I was so broken.

KATHIE LEE: Men sense the vulnerability. So how were you feeling about all this attention? Was it flattering?

ANNE FERRELL: No, I couldn't have cared less. Diane kept saying, "Are you not seeing this?" And I was like, "No." I didn't even notice it because I was so broken.

KATHIE LEE: So you weren't on the prowl at all?

ANNE FERRELL: Oh no. Remember, I hadn't told anyone about my struggle in my marriage. Diane had no idea I'd been unhappy. So the whole weekend was sort of "We're just going to have fun."

KATHIE LEE: Like shopping and getting your nails done? Things like that?

ANNE FERRELL: Exactly. So we went to dinner one night. Diane started saying, "That guy keeps staring at you." I was like, "Whatever." We kept talking, and she was like, "Look, there he is. He's back." I looked up at this man, and he came over and introduced himself. He had a thick accent, and he was handsome. When he sat down, it was like everything I said was the funniest thing he'd ever heard or the smartest thing he'd ever heard or the most interesting thing he'd ever heard. And I went from this wilted little flower with weeds all around, and I just emerged—

KATHIE LEE: You blossomed?

ANNE FERRELL: I totally blossomed right before his eyes. And of course, it was incredibly confusing.

KATHIE LEE: Right, so what did you do?

ANNE FERRELL: Well, here's what happened sort of in generalities. I began, basically, a three-year affair. I knew what I was doing was wrong, but I didn't want anyone to know. That started my secret life.

KATHIE LEE: How were you seeing him?

ANNE FERRELL: Well, he was very wealthy, and he would arrange for me to see him. So I would live my normal life, and then I had my double life. I was going to church every Sunday with a smile on my face and my daughters with their bows in their hair, and no one knew the double life I was leading. At that time, Bob didn't go to church very often. But it became clear I had gotten Bob's attention. He said, "Let's go to counseling."

I agreed to go to counseling with him for one reason, and it was really selfish. In my mind, God had provided this great person who was totally in love with me, gave me all this attention, and provided everything. I was convinced this was from God. But if I just left Bob outright, people would look at me and say, "How did she just walk off and leave her husband?" So I decided, "I'll go to counseling with Bob and pretend like I'm working on our relationship," *wink-wink*, knowing I wasn't in love with him and I was going to move on.

KATHIE LEE: You were planning on marrying this new man?

ANNE FERRELL: Oh yeah, I had my whole life planned out. But when I look back, I can see God's hand even in my counseling, which I went to for looks.

KATHIE LEE: Just for the perception?

ANNE FERRELL: Yes. God used that counseling—it really got Bob's attention. Bob was finally like, "What do I need to do?" Even the counselor said, "Your wife has one foot out the door, and you are not getting it." He didn't get it really until then.

And I remember my personal counselor, whom I was still seeing during our couples' counseling: I asked her, "Do you really believe I can fall in love with Bob again?" She said, "I do."

KATHIE LEE: "With God all things are possible."

ANNE FERRELL: Yes. So we went to couples' counseling, and I saw how hard Bob was trying. He started saying, "I've arranged for a babysitter. How about we go out?" He started courting me.

KATHIE LEE: He courted you again!

ANNE FERRELL: Yes, and he was such a gentleman. He let me move at my own pace. And I started falling for him again.

KATHIE LEE: Did he know about the affair at that time?

ANNE FERRELL: Nope, he had no idea. And you know what I think is so interesting, Kathie? Our story is an illustration of allowing the Holy Spirit to do the work. Nobody was putting their finger in my face, saying, "You sinner, you bad person." No one knew. It was the Holy Spirit working in my heart.

KATHIE LEE: So what did you say to the other man when he tried to see you?

ANNE FERRELL: I started making excuses why I couldn't see him. I wanted to break up with the other man, but it wasn't as easy as I thought. This is the thing that's very serious about sin, when you entangle yourself in sin. I got really entangled.

KATHIE LEE: You had a soul tie with this man.

ANNE FERRELL: I just couldn't break it off. And especially toward the end, it was hard because I was in so deep. And this is another thing where God really revealed Himself. You know Psalm 139, the one that says, "Where can I flee from Your presence?"

KATHIE LEE: Yes. God is everywhere.

ANNE FERRELL: At that point, I was deep into my sexual sin, and I wanted to get out. Yet God was there. I remember thinking, "*I need to call my mom.*" But I knew every time I called my parents, my mom would say,

"Let me get your father on the line." And it took me about a week to get up the courage to call them because my dad's a lot like Billy Graham.

KATHIE LEE: Yeah, and you don't want to tell Billy Graham you're having an affair!

ANNE FERRELL: But I knew I needed them to help me get out of this. Finally, I was so desperate, I called my mom. She said, "Oh, honey, your father is not here. Can you call back?" I said, "Mom, actually, you're the one I want to talk to."

And, Kathie, I was just sobbing, saying, "I'm having an affair. I can't get out." And my mom said everything a mom should say. At the end of the conversation, she said, "Honey, you know I need to tell your father," and I said, "I know." She said, "Let me talk to him overnight, and call us back tomorrow. We're going to help you get out of this."

KATHIE LEE: That's a real parent. Such loving parents.

ANNE FERRELL: The next day, I called back. And my dad got on the phone. The first thing he said was, "Anne Ferrell, you are loved, and you are forgiven. You are going to be okay. We want to help you." So they helped me deal with it. They said, "The first thing you have to do is call this man and say, 'No more.'"

But of course, the man didn't want to let me go so easy. So my parents said, "Every time he says anything, you call us, and we will help you." My parents helped me break it off. I ended it with him, and my parents never told anyone.

Then I felt the Holy Spirit telling me to change churches. I had kind of a religious spirit where I thought you had to be Presbyterian. That's why I'd told Bob, "I won't marry Catholic."

KATHIE LEE: Oh yes. And that didn't work out too well!

ANNE FERRELL: But I really felt like God was like, "*Let's look at church.*" And Kathie, you always say it's not a religion; it's a relationship. The Holy Spirit was trying to teach me that, and He took me to an Episcopal church where they have the liturgy. I started going, and Bob started going with me. We started going as a family. And the rector was teaching a class on forgiveness. So Bob would go home after service, and I'd stay at church with the girls and go to this class on forgiveness. And it was just like laser darts right into my heart.

I made an appointment to see the rector and confessed everything. I told him the affair had ended and I was healing, but I was worried about my guilt and my shame. And one thing I love about a liturgical church, there's a prayer of penance. We prayed together, and I was sobbing. When I went home that night, I started reading my Bible. I had never really read Psalm 51, after David and Bathsheba. And David said, "If you take away my guilt, I will teach the transgressors," something to that effect. I knew God took away my shame and my guilt. And I realized God was telling me I needed to be open about my story. And the beautiful thing that came out of this is, there's a verse in Isaiah that says after your double portion of shame, you'll have a double portion of blessing. Bob and I had two more children.

KATHIE LEE: The four children you said you were going to have!

ANNE FERRELL: Yeah, yes. And I ended with the Preston. Robert is my Preston.

KATHIE LEE: So sweet!

ANNE FERRELL: Bob didn't know the whole story though. When I look back, I see God's hand in everything. As Bob and I were working it out, he would occasionally say, "Anne Ferrell, there's more to that time when you wanted to leave, isn't there?" And I would say, "Bob, if you want to know, I'll tell you." And he would say, "No, I don't need to know." So that went on for several years.

Then in 2009, my dad was dying of cancer. I went back to Florida to spend time with him. And during that time, I finally told Bob all the details even though he didn't really ask. I needed to tell him about what my dad had done for me.

When I told Bob the whole story, do you know what he said? Now at this point, this was fifteen years after the affair, and we were doing great. We had our kids; we were thriving. But when he heard all of it, he said, "Anne Ferrell, I'm so sorry I wasn't there for you."

KATHIE LEE: Oh, sweetheart.

ANNE FERRELL: So that's the story.

KATHIE LEE: Yeah. So when you think back on that whole episode, is it hard to believe that was even you?

ANNE FERRELL: One hundred percent. But you know what it also did? Growing up, I was legalistic. I was so rigid about the rules. After I told my sister about the affair, she said, "I've got to be honest with you. I like you so much better now." Now I have compassion and empathy and am not judgmental. I'm like, "Who am I to judge?"

KATHIE LEE: There but for the grace of God go I.

ANNE FERRELL: Exactly.

KATHIE LEE: And it was the grace of God that brought you through. And you rediscovered the love of your life.

ANNE FERRELL: Yeah, exactly.

KATHIE LEE: But Bob had to rediscover the kind of husband he needed to be to you.

ANNE FERRELL: Right, right.

KATHIE LEE: Well, it was precious of you to share your story with me, sweetheart. You're brave, and I love you for sharing it. You know you're forgiven, and Bob knows he's forgiven. And I'm so glad that you have such a happy ending to this story since so many of them don't end this way.

ANNE FERRELL: Yeah. You can understand not only my passion for Bob but also my passion for Jesus.

KATHIE LEE: Yes. Well, I love you for it. Such a great story, honey, thank you.

SEVEN

JESUS AS A SOFT PLACE TO FALL

MEGYN KELLY

Most of America has become familiar with the beautiful, brilliant journalist and attorney Megyn Kelly since she came on the scene on Fox News Channel and immediately made a name for herself in the cutthroat world of cable news.

I first met Megyn through the nonprofit Childhelp, when I gave her the media award for shining a critical light on the issue of child abuse and neglect. I already respected her, but I immediately liked her as well. But it wasn't until years later that I got the chance to spend enough time with her to get a window into her soul.

When it was announced that Megyn had been hired by NBC to host an hour-long talk show during the *Today* show, it set tongues wagging. Having decades of experience navigating the treacherous nature of morning television at ABC with Regis and NBC with Hoda, I knew Megyn was in for a difficult and potentially devastating experience. So I called her to express my welcome to *Today* and extend an invitation to join me every Tuesday for lunch at my favorite restaurant, Neary's pub, where she would be safe from prying eyes and overhearing ears. We spent about six weeks together weathering her storm, and it bonded our new friendship in a very special way.

Rarely has Megyn given the world a glimpse of what she believes spiritually. I think you will be as moved as I am.

KATHIE LEE: I'm interested in talking to people who have an interesting life story to tell. I'd love to know your first recollection about Jesus. I know you grew up in a Catholic home, but I don't know if you were raised in the Catholic faith. So tell me, what did you know of Jesus as a child?

MEGYN: My family was Catholic, and we were observant. My dad, who grew up in Brooklyn, thought he wanted to become a priest. He had a Catholic education and was on his way to becoming a Catholic priest when he met my mom. She put an end to that. He was only twenty when he met my mom. Sadly, my dad died suddenly when I was in high school. Years later, my mom got remarried, and Peter had also once intended on becoming a priest. There's something about these religious men that attracts my mom, and my mom, too, was very observant. My nana was a convert. She'd grown up Lutheran, and then she met my pop pop, who was fresh off the boat from Italy, so truly Catholic. She converted to Catholicism. And like most converts, she meant it. So she had my mom going to church religiously every Sunday and observing all the rites of passage, and my mom did the same with us.

I would say when I was going through all of that, I wasn't so much learning about Scripture and the Psalms. I was learning more about ethics. That was my biggest takeaway: "How does Jesus want me to behave? Why are we here every Sunday?" It wasn't so much about the biblical history. I always feel like when people start quoting Bible verses, I'm a little lost.

My dad was an education professor when the priest thing didn't work out, and he used to have other professors and PhD students to our house all the time. They'd discuss philosophy and religion once a week, and we'd be sitting there with guys with beards and guitars talking about Jesus, and that's what I remember. That's how I feel like

I learned about who He was and why He mattered to me. And why it was something I could consider following, or emulating, and consider believing in terms of His messaging. It was societal, yes, because we went to church, but it was closer to home that really did it for me.

KATHIE LEE: And what did Jesus represent to you? You believed He was a historical person?

MEGYN: Yes, of course. My dad used to say, "You can't understand Jesus unless you can picture Him as a man. As vulnerable and human as any man." He used to say that, for example, in the throes of sexual attraction. He was trying to tell us that the point is Jesus wasn't just the Son of God. He was teaching us that He was someone who understood us because He was also one of us, and that makes His goals for us more achievable. He's not just Christ, whose standards you could never meet. He was fallible because He was human. He was a man and, therefore, accessible. That's the messaging that my dad used to bring.

KATHIE LEE: Wow. Did he believe that Jesus was without sin? The Bible does say that Jesus was in all ways tempted as we are but without sin.

MEGYN: Yes. Without sin but tempted.

KATHIE LEE: So as you went through your life, was prayer real to you?

MEGYN: Of course. I prayed all the time. In fact, still one of my favorite times is after you get Communion in the Catholic Church you go back to the pew, get on your knees, and pray. It's an expected part of the Mass. It's private prayer and your moment not to be listening to the priest, not to be saying "peace" with fellow congregants. It's just between you and God in that moment, you and Jesus. That was an appointment between me and Jesus every week. And then, of course, I said my prayers every night in my bed, which my kids do now. We say grace every night as a family. So prayer was incorporated, but I wouldn't say in the way that you do it. Every time you say a prayer, I'm blown away by how natural it is and what a good conversation you have with God just off the top of your head. I don't think I'm good at it that way, but it's a soft place to fall and that's really how I see Jesus. He is my soft place to fall.

KATHIE LEE: Were there any times that you doubted Him? You went through some very hard times in your life. Was Jesus always present with you?

MEGYN: I feel like there have been only two lanes in which I've doubted Jesus, and it was never with tragedies that happened to me. I've wrestled, like most Christians, with, "Why is there cancer? Why is there war? Why is there suffering for babies and children? How could God allow this?" And then the separate lane is when I listen to someone like Sam Harris—he's a philosopher who is an atheist. And when I listen to him talk about religion, it can be persuasive. He can pull you to this place of "This whole thing is a terrible ruse." You go and watch *The Book of Mormon*, and you can think, *Oh my gosh, is this all made up? Is it all a delusion?* But for me, the course correction to both of those lanes is always real life. Your own experience. You see your first ultrasound; you see the perfect curve of your child's face while he's asleep. You see a tragedy. I just spoke with Eric Bolling, whose son died at age nineteen of an accidental overdose. But then you see that parent pick himself up and carry on and help others after one of the most terrible tragedies and find happiness again. And that's when you know there's something else powering this.

I always come back to, "This cannot be all biology and cells and physics." And even the Sam Harrises of the world, as brilliant as they are, are mere mortals. Who are they to say definitively there is nothing more? Where is our humility? How can we know it isn't true? For me, my heart, my life experience, my joy is when I'm in communication with Christ. That tells me He does exist. He died for me. And thanks to Him, I have everlasting life, and my loved ones do. And the world, while it has its flaws, has been turned into an infinitely better place.

KATHIE LEE: Thank you. That's beautiful. I knew your faith had an impact on you, but you're so poetic and lovely in your expression of it.

MEGYN: I kind of liked this assignment. It was a fun exercise. And it makes me feel better about my life and my relationship with Jesus.

KATHIE LEE: I do think we need Him more than ever. What happened to grace, forgiveness, mercy—all those things we were taught? And he who is without sin cast the first stone? Some people believe that Jesus, when He was writing in the dust in John 8, He was writing the names of the accusers who had sinned with the woman caught in adultery. We don't know for sure, but many scholars believe that's what He was doing.

MEGYN: The more we push Him out of the public square, the more we fill it with totally banal things: worship of self, of money, power. All these fleeting things that are ultimately meaningless and not fulfilling at all.

KATHIE LEE: They do not lead to the nirvana that they promise.

MEGYN: We have all these suicides of famous rich people. Hollywood is not the answer. Money's not either. We're putting our focus on the wrong place.

KATHIE LEE: The problem today is not Jesus; it's His followers.

MEGYN: It's manifesting. People talk about cancel culture, yes, but it's so much bigger than that. You've pushed out the number-one Person you need to be thinking about, the one who is the solution to what's really ailing us.

KATHIE LEE: God did not leave us; we left Him. We pushed Him out.

MEGYN: They made fun of O'Reilly with his "war on Christmas." It was emblematic of a bigger rejection of faith in America—part of our country's foundation. It was the bedrock. I mean, look at the Declaration of Independence. We're going in the opposite direction now, and it's scary. I don't know how to stop it.

KATHIE LEE: The word *repentance* means "to turn around." Turn around and come home to Abba Father.

MEGYN: You've said when you live vertically, things go well. When you live horizontally, not so well. I love that. It's a good, easy, linear way of thinking about it.

KATHIE LEE: As your morning goes, your day goes and your life goes. If I start my day out with the first love of my life, Jesus, I'm connected. I don't have to go looking for Him when I need Him during the day.

MEGYN: You truly are an example to all of us. You have made a difference for me.

EIGHT

A MOTHER'S PRAYERS FOR JUSTIN BIEBER

PATTIE MALLETTE

Pattie Mallette is best known for being Justin Bieber's mother. I first met her when I interviewed her for the *Today* show about her book, *Nowhere but Up*. She has lived a lot of life for a woman who gave birth to Justin when she was practically still a child herself. I talked with her about how her faith in Jesus has influenced her not only as a person but also as the mother of a superstar.

KATHIE LEE: You were a child basically when you gave birth to a child, right? Take us back.

PATTIE: I think I was eighteen when I got pregnant with him.

KATHIE LEE: Where were you in your state of mind and in your circumstances when you were pregnant with the person the world would come to know as the superstar Justin Bieber? Of course, you had no idea at that time. You were a frightened teenager in Canada.

PATTIE: I had just given my life to God six months earlier. I was in the hospital for trying to commit suicide, and I encountered God there. Before that time, I had been groomed for abortion, and I fought on prochoice debates. But after I met Jesus, I started really trying to get to know God, really learning about Him, going to church, growing in my faith. And I decided to try to let all my old friends know about God. So I started hanging back out with my party friends. And next thing you know, I was back in my old ways, and I found myself high and drunk and pregnant.

I was so ashamed to come back to a church as an unwed mom, but they loved me and encouraged me and told me, "When you fall down, you just have to get back up again." They taught me about the mercy of God and the forgiveness of Jesus. And so I knew when I got pregnant it wasn't okay for me to have an abortion. I knew it wasn't okay in God's eyes, and it wouldn't have been okay between me and God if I were to do that. Though I was not prepared, I decided to trust God and go ahead and give birth to my son and try the best I could to raise him.

KATHIE LEE: And the strength that you got was from your community of believers?

PATTIE: They were really healthy, a great church the way you would hope God's church would be. They loved me unconditionally. They didn't coddle me; they didn't encourage destructive behavior. They modeled grace and forgiveness and God's mercy and encouraged me to keep coming back to God and doing the best that I can with what He gives me and letting Him make up the difference with the rest.

KATHIE LEE: So this little angel boy comes into your life. What was your relationship with his father at that time?

PATTIE: Jeremy and I had a little bit of a toxic relationship. We were on again, off again, just really wounded and not ready for the responsibility of adulthood.

KATHIE LEE: How old was he when you had Justin?

PATTIE: I was eighteen, so he would've been nineteen.

KATHIE LEE: Children having children. And did he encourage you to have an abortion, or was he supportive of you giving birth?

PATTIE: I had a lot of pressure to have an abortion, but Jeremy never pressured me in that way. I really want to honor Jeremy. He's come a long way, and I've come a long way.

KATHIE LEE: I love the growth in you now. Do you have a sense that everything that you went through at that time was actually meant to be to bring forth the greater good in bringing this young man into the world who's changing the world in many ways?

PATTIE: I do believe that God uses everything the enemy means for evil and turns it around for good. Our selfishness and our sin and the things the devil would try to throw at us, He does use it all for our good. He's amazing.

KATHIE LEE: So then this little one comes into the world. Take me back to that first moment you saw him in your arms.

PATTIE: I was so filled with shame that I had to ask God to have mercy and give him ten fingers and ten toes and let him be healthy. But in God's incredible mercy, it was far more than I could ever imagine. He did more than that. He made him gifted in every imaginable way. Justin was perfect and beautiful, and I remember him crying and it sounded like singing. It was really special.

KATHIE LEE: And so then you were struggling as a single mom. At what age did you notice he was so gifted?

PATTIE: I think he was playing drums in my stomach! He was very gifted in rhythm, so even in his high chair he would bang to the beat to copy drum riffs. By the time he was two, he was playing a 4/4 beat with music on a drum set we got him. We got him a little hand *djembe*, keyboards. He was always playing with instruments at a young age.

KATHIE LEE: In the meantime, were you growing as a Christian, or were you still battling your former demons?

PATTIE: I think we're always growing as Christians and battling our former demons!

KATHIE LEE: I know I still am!

PATTIE: This is a journey, and God's mercies are new every morning, gratefully. And He works in us according to His good pleasure, so we're being transformed into His image. I'm always growing and learning and trying to be better. There have been some ups and downs and some hard times and easier times to bring times of refreshing. I think He's faithful. He's doing the work. We just have to surrender and say yes, and He does the rest.

KATHIE LEE: The Lord's been placing on my heart the past few months that the first three letters of Jesus' Hebrew name *Yeshua* are *Yes*. So, yes, Yeshua. Okay, so tell me about the mother in you. You raised Justin to love Jesus; you instilled in Justin the knowledge of his Savior and who Jesus was. When he rebelled and was seduced by the industry, what were your fears for him then?

PATTIE: The Bible says you raise a child "in the way he should go, and when he is old he will not depart from it." And so I trusted God. I did my best to love him and asked God to love him through me. I raised him in the way he should go, and God affirmed me—when we went down this road of pursuing Justin's music and his career—that I could trust Him. I had dedicated his life to God when he was a baby, and I had to trust God. Our children are not our own. They're on loan to us. We're just responsible to lead them the best way we can and let God make up the difference. I've just really done my best to continue to bring Justin before Him and pray for His will to be done in his life. Justin has free will, but he has chosen to make Jesus Lord and Savior, and God is gonna be the one to reveal to him the truth. The Bible says that He will teach all our children, "and great will be their peace."

KATHIE LEE: What was the lowest point during that time when he was rebelling, struggling, and it was so public?

PATTIE: I don't know. There were a few really tough times when he was struggling with addiction and substance abuse. It's really scary because there are things driving a person who has addiction to substances to self-medicate, and they're not in their right mind. And I was worried about him doing damage to himself and to others. No mother likes to see her child arrested or shamed in any way. I don't know how many mothers experience their kids going through public shame. It's definitely not fun to watch. It's tough letting your children make their own mistakes and letting go in some ways to figure some things out when they don't want your advice and don't want your opinions, and you have to trust God.

KATHIE LEE: My daddy used to say, "I love you too much to deny you the privilege of making mistakes." That's a good saying until it's your kid who's making the mistakes. During all of this, though, Pattie, you've become known to the world as Justin Bieber's mother. But you were your own person before you gave birth to him, and you are your own person, your own woman, since you gave birth to him. So where is that person right now? Pattie, the child of God, daughter of the King, where is she right now?

PATTIE: She's still a child of God. I think for me Jesus is always the prize. It doesn't matter where we're going or what we're doing. He gets better every day. He makes life bearable. It's all for Him. It's all to Him, it's all about Him, and He loves me. And I think it's hard for people who don't know God and don't know His love to relate to His love.

KATHIE LEE: That's why the world looks like it looks right now. They don't know that God loves them and has a plan and a purpose for their lives beyond anything they could ever dream. But don't you sense now, not only in your own life but in Justin's—now he's married to a godly girl, and they seem to be truly in love and devoted to each other—are you just full of hope for the future? Or do you still have doubts? Satan knows our most vulnerable spots. Is that the thing you have to come against the most?

PATTIE: It depends on the season. I think Satan is always throwing different things at us. I think he tries to attack our identity and tell us that we're not worthy, we're less than, that we don't matter, that our voices don't matter, our lives don't matter. The Bible says the devil comes to steal, kill, and destroy, so the negative voices and the things that are telling us the opposite of what God has to say to us are really what we're fighting against.

KATHIE LEE: What is the biggest lesson you've learned in all these years of walking with your Savior Jesus?

PATTIE: The biggest lesson I've learned is that God is faithful even when we are not, and His ways are not our ways. And that He has good plans for us. It may not be what we want, when we want, how we want, or what we think it's going to look like, but He's good and He really does know what's best for us. He's shown Himself faithful time and time and time again.

KATHIE LEE: And going forward, if your life were a mission statement, what would it be?

PATTIE: That's a good one. I don't know. God is love.

KATHIE LEE: That's perfect. If only the world knew that! What has surprised you the most about Jesus?

PATTIE: I think His mercy, His goodness, His kindness.

KATHIE LEE: And what are your hopes for the future?

PATTIE: Right now, I'm on a little bit of a hiatus. COVID has really thrown everybody for a loop. It's put a lot of people in a forced rest. I'm trying to heal and rest and create and prepare for what's next. I've been healing up from my past and the whirlwind of Justin Bieber Land, and I think now He's preparing me for my next season and calling me forward. And I'm trying to get thicker skin because I know that if the world hated Jesus, then they're going to hate us, too, who represent Him. And we love the world enough to tell them the truth and be hated for it, in the hopes that some would come to know the mercy and the truth of who God is for eternity.

NINE

CALLING JESUS ON THE MAIN LINE

JIMMIE ALLEN

During my decades in the entertainment industry, I have met many brilliantly talented performers. Some I could tell were destined to have huge, enduring careers the minute I heard them or watched them perform: Celine Dion, the first time I heard her rehearsing in the *Live with Regis and Kathie Lee* studio at 6:00 a.m; Justin Timberlake, when he first guested with me and Regis as a part of NSYNC; and Jimmie Allen, when he made his national television debut singing his first hit country single on *Today* with me and Hoda.

Jimmie is an electric, spontaneous, combustible force of nature who can do it all. We have worked a lot together in the last few years, and I hope we will continue to find new projects long into the future. Buckle up for this one, folks! You're in for quite a ride!

KATHIE LEE: I know you grew up in Delaware. Tell me about the home you grew up in.

JIMMIE: I grew up in this little town. It was cool. We grew up doing stuff that a lot of country people do, whether that's fishing, hunting. My dad didn't really go to church. My mom and me and my sisters went a lot.

KATHIE LEE: What church was it, sweetie?

JIMMIE: It was this church called Mount Carmel. It was cool, but I kind of got to a point going so much, I got burned-out. I needed a break.

KATHIE LEE: At what age did you feel that way?

JIMMIE: Thirteen. And then at eighteen I stopped going to church, and I didn't go again. I didn't step foot in church again until I was twenty-seven.

KATHIE LEE: What happened?

JIMMIE: I just got burned-out. It felt like, "What's the difference between going to church and believing in God?" But here is the thing, to me the church is just a building. So it's like, you go and sit there all day, listening to some dude just talk and talk. And there's no real interaction, you know what I mean?

I thought, "*This ain't fun. This is miserable.*" I was sitting there every Sunday from nine o'clock until the main service started at eleven. We got out at two, then we went back for the afternoon. It just felt like so much pressure and felt like every little thing you do you will get sent to hell for. I was like, "What kind of God is this?" They took the words "fear God" out of context; they actually feared Him. To me, the words "fear God" mean reverence, respect.

KATHIE LEE: Yep, that's exactly right.

JIMMIE: Not "fear" as in terrified. And I feel like that's how a lot of modern-day believers use that phrase, as in, "You fear Him because He can smite you." And I'm like, "Well, if the God you're telling me about forces you to do what He says, why do you need to have a relationship with Him?" So that's kind of what I struggled with for a long time.

KATHIE LEE: And what did your mom say to that? Because she was the biggest influence on your spiritual life, right?

JIMMIE: Yeah, my mom said, "Jimmie, all that I do is teach you what I know, and you make your own decisions." She never tried to force God or Jesus on me. Some people try to shove faith down your throat, and I'm like, "You're doing more harm than good." You know what I mean?

KATHIE LEE: Yeah, of course.

JIMMIE: God always finds a way to show up in a person's life to where they make a decision if they want a relationship with Him or not. I think it's our job to encourage each other, right? Then once we get to a certain point, God takes His man.

KATHIE LEE: And your mom was praying for you, right? She may not have been forcing anything down your throat, but that woman—I've met her, and that is a praying mother.

JIMMIE: Oh yeah, she was praying for me. It's cool to have her as a mom and the things she taught me.

KATHIE LEE: And where was your dad during this time, sweetheart?

JIMMIE: My dad didn't go to church at all. He was like, "Yeah, God is real. But no, man, I'm not going to sit in this building all day." I still agree with that to this day; just because God is there does not mean we have to be sitting in a church building all day. I feel like people sometimes get so wrapped up in church, they forget what God is about. You know, a lot of people claim they want to be like God, but no one is actually doing what God did. Nobody is taking the time to actually show God's love to people, you know what I mean.

KATHIE LEE: Real, oh yeah.

JIMMIE: Yeah, the real thing.

KATHIE LEE: Now between the ages of eighteen and twenty-seven, before you came back to church, what were you doing in those years?

JIMMIE: I was building my career. I was just hanging out, partying, doing music.

KATHIE LEE: Where did you go?

JIMMIE: I was in Nashville. I went to Nashville when I was twenty-one.

KATHIE LEE: Started working odd jobs and playing gigs?

JIMMIE: Yeah, I just started working jobs playing at different bars. Anywhere I could play, chasing music, jamming, doing commercials here and there.

KATHIE LEE: Did you get caught up in a bit of the "I got to do whatever it takes to make my dreams come true"? How were you feeling then about everything?

JIMMIE: I felt great. I don't really get wrapped up in stuff. So, for me, it was like, "Okay, I want to work at this place, great." And then, "I'm going to meet this person. I want to go drink for a while, I want to party, I want to go hang out and sleep with this girl." Then once I decided I was done, I just shut it off. That's just how my brain works. So that's why I want life experiences. Like, you have really sheltered Christians who just regurgitate what their parents taught them, but they haven't experienced life at all, to a point where sometimes they don't have a relationship with God themselves. They have their parents' relationship with God. I feel like you can love God, but you don't quite understand how much He loves you and His mercy until you get yourself jammed up.

KATHIE LEE: And did you get jammed up?

JIMMIE: Yeah, I got jammed up. At one time I thought I had four girls pregnant. Come to find out, none of them was pregnant, but I didn't know that yet. I was stressed-out. I was like, "Oh my God, I got four women pregnant."

KATHIE LEE: You can barely feed yourself, and you might have to feed four babies?

JIMMIE: Tell me about it. I was waiting tables at the time. It was a mess. But in that moment, I was like, "Man, well, I gotta give God a holler real quick." That's how it started, it was like, "Man, I am jammed up, let me holler at You real quick."

KATHIE LEE: And what happened when you called out?

JIMMIE: So I reached out, like the old black gospel song, "Jesus on the main line. Tell Him what you want." So I called Jesus up on the main line, and I was like, "Hey, man, I have a situation. I am in a pickle." I was like, "Listen, I need You to get me out of this thing."

KATHIE LEE: And did you feel close to Him then?

JIMMIE: No, that's not how it started. It was just like, "I need You to get me out of a pickle." And I said, "I'll go to church every week, I'll get a relationship with You, just help me out this one time." And God knew I was just doing that to get out. So He helped me out. I still didn't set foot in the church. I went right back to what I was doing. Then I got in another pickle, and I called on Him again. And I reneged on everything I promised the second time. I called on Him again when I got in another pickle, and He showed up again.

KATHIE LEE: I'm glad you didn't lose His number!

JIMMIE: After that, I was sitting home one day by myself. And I was just thinking about, I was having a hard time trying to find friends. I was like, "*Man, I can't count on nobody.*" Then it hit me: God had been there for me every time in the midst of my craziness, making promises He knew I wasn't going to keep, but He still came through. And that right there is what changed my whole relationship with God, seeing everything He had done for me and how He was always there, even when He knew I was going to stab Him in the back. He knew what was going on, but He said, "I'm going to help him out."

KATHIE LEE: Oh, Jimmie, you are so sweet!

JIMMIE: And I know everybody has a different story, but for me I wasn't just going to follow this whole God thing because that's what I was raised to do. Or because that's what my friends did. I needed to see this for myself in order for me to believe. You know what I mean?

KATHIE LEE: Like the doubting Thomas?

JIMMIE: Yeah, it's easy for people who have a relationship with God to tell people who don't have one, "You just got to believe." I said, "No, something in your life happened for you to believe. Why don't I get that same experience? I want that experience you had to where God became real for you." I feel like we all have different journeys, and it's impossible to reach people on the other side of the fence if you've never been there. Sometimes I feel like God allowed me to spiral out of control for a while because I can actually have a conversation and communicate with people who are in that, because I've experienced it.

KATHIE LEE: God has not wasted all these experiences on you. You're able to apply them now in relationships with others, yeah.

JIMMIE: I'm not saying go do all that. I'm just saying don't be afraid of your scars. I once heard this great analogy. This guy took out a twenty-dollar bill and said to a girl, "This twenty-dollar bill is you. If I dropped the twenty-dollar bill, and I give it to you, would you still want it?" The girl said, "Yes." He said, "If I crumple this twenty-dollar bill and throw it across the room, you still want it?" "Yes." "If I threw dirt all over the twenty-dollar bill, would you still want it?" She said, "Yes." He said, "That's how we are. No matter how damaged we are, we never lose our value."

KATHIE LEE: Yeah, great analogy.

JIMMIE: We just got to remember that in the midst of our mess-ups, our shortcomings, and trying to figure out who we are, to God, we never lose our value.

KATHIE LEE: So true. So at that point you come through the haze a bit. Tell me about that.

JIMMIE: Yeah, I went to church. They met on Saturday afternoons. I loved it because it was convenient. I was like, "Man, I want to go to church, but I still want to go out Friday nights and Saturday nights."

KATHIE LEE: Of course.

JIMMIE: They had this group called Friday Night Lights. I remember I walked in church one day, a few people my age came on to say, "Hey, we got this group of friends that like to hang with us." I'm like, "Man, I won't do Bible study." And they were like, "It's not really Bible study, just people to do life with." And I went, and that's what changed my life. I'm still friends with them today. We would get together, we read a little Scripture, and we would just talk about life. That's what felt like church was designed to be—people to walk through life with.

KATHIE LEE: That's how the first church started, definitely. There was no building.

JIMMIE: Friday Night Lights is what really turned it around for me. Because I had this image in my head where, "Man, Christians can't have a beer. Christians can't get angry." And I was like, "When I get upset, I like to have a beer, so I guess I don't belong in the God followers." But they showed me how to be a real person, to have a relationship with God. To fall but know you can still get back up.

KATHIE LEE: He will help us up, right.

JIMMIE: Yeah. That's what changed my life.

KATHIE LEE: And so, at this point, you're in a relationship with a woman, and you have a child together, right?

JIMMIE: Well, it didn't start off as a relationship. We were just hanging out, and it kind of turned into one. Then my son was born, and, you know, we separated, called it quits. And then I just started working on me, trying to figure out what I wanted in life.

KATHIE LEE: How did that baby change you, sweetie? Tell us about that.

JIMMIE: Knowing I was responsible for him. I was like, "All right, it's my job to now equip him with everything he needs in life. Not only street smarts, school smarts, but also relation with God. I have to show him who God is." I felt like as a parent, it's my obligation to introduce God to him. So that way, my son knows who He is; God isn't a stranger.

KATHIE LEE: Right. Like your mother did for you?

JIMMIE: Oh yeah. She still does.

KATHIE LEE: Yeah, sure. And so you have this precious little boy, and your career is starting to soar. By that time, you had your first number-one single and were just about to put out your second one, is that right?

JIMMIE: Yes. I was just working wherever I could. And then I got a publishing deal in 2016 and a record deal in 2017. And, you know, everything was shifting. But that's when I finally got a grasp on who I was as a man.

KATHIE LEE: And as an artist?

JIMMIE: And as an artist—that was the biggest point, trying to figure that out. "Who am I as an artist, what do I want to say, what's my purpose?" And I felt like having my son really helped me look forward.

KATHIE LEE: And now you're happily married to the gorgeous Lexie, and you have your little daughter. Tell me how that all came to be.

JIMMIE: Well, we knew about each other for a while. We're from the same hometown. My cousin's a friend of her parents. So they were trying to hook us up a couple years before, but I just wasn't in the right place, and I was still doing my things. We kind of just started hanging out, formed a relationship, and got engaged, got married, had a daughter. It was the right time. I felt like she was the right person, but timing was very important.

KATHIE LEE: Right. So now when you look back at your life, what would you say to that little boy today that you know now as Jimmie Allen, the man?

JIMMIE: I would tell him, "Don't be afraid of your mistakes. Don't let people convince you that you're not worth anything because of the bad choices you made. You'll find your way through and use your bad choices as lessons to learn from. Work to get better every day because you'll get to that point."

KATHIE LEE: And how would you describe Jesus in your life today, sweetie?

JIMMIE: Today, He's like a big brother, somebody who's always there for me. But now I don't just call Him when I'm in trouble. I just talk to build that relationship. He's someone I can talk to when things are going great and also when things are going bad.

KATHIE LEE: Yeah, He's the constant compass, right?

JIMMIE: *Constant*, that word is so important.

KATHIE LEE: When everything else is changing all around us, He never changes. You'll have hits, you'll be played on the radio, and then you'll probably get a great song you think is going to be it, and it's not going to be, but what's the constant? Jesus, always Jesus.

TEN

A NEW PART OF THE FAMILY

GRANT GASTON

I met Grant recently when he moved into a hotel nearby. My best friend in Tennessee, Angie Clawson, and I began to include him in all our activities because that's what Angie does. She welcomes you into the neighborhood, and then she adopts you.

Little did Grant know that meeting Angie would begin the journey of a lifetime, far beyond his native Australia.

KATHIE LEE: You've been sweet enough to agree to share your story. I know you grew up in Australia. Did you grow up in a faith kind of a home?

GRANT: I did. My father was a schoolteacher in a little country town, and we used to go to the local Presbyterian church.

KATHIE LEE: So were your parents what you would call religious people?

GRANT: My mother probably more so than my father, yeah, definitely.

KATHIE LEE: And what did she tell you about God when you were growing up?

GRANT: I can't remember her saying anything specific because it was really just going to church. It was all about being a leader and setting the standards and values and morality.

KATHIE LEE: Okay. A lot of people use church as a code of ethics, basically, to raise their children. So let's fast-forward. What brought you to America, and why particularly Tennessee?

GRANT: I had the master franchise for Australia, New Zealand, for a big health-care brand. But the Australian health-care system is very different than the one in the USA because it is government funded.

KATHIE LEE: So you ended up at a convention where you met a woman?

GRANT: Yeah. I attended a conference in Austin, Texas, and I came across a business opportunity with a lady who had developed this marketing system. I decided that her marketing system sounded great, so I'd take it back to Australia. Part of that was wanting to get to know her better but also flying her out to Australia to help me run my first Australian franchise conference.

KATHIE LEE: So you went into business with her?

GRANT: I went into business with her while I was still in Australia. Then I decided to move to the USA. So she became my sponsor, and we set up a company in the USA. It was business, but it also turned into love. When I did finally move to Tennessee, we shared a house together. And we shared the business together.

KATHIE LEE: And did you think that would be forever?

GRANT: I'd hoped, and we'd talked a lot about that. But a lot of business things got in the way.

KATHIE LEE: Okay, so suddenly that relationship ended. What were you feeling at that point? I mean, you were a long way from home, and you were separated from your son. You never did marry her, right?

GRANT: No.

KATHIE LEE: Okay, so what were you feeling then?

GRANT: There was a lot of guilt around what I had left behind, my family being left behind in Australia, particularly my son, who was nineteen at the time.

KATHIE LEE: Did you feel like you were abandoning him?

GRANT: My son was coming here quite a bit, so that was great. But now when I reflect on it, I'm not sure what I was trying to do. I think I was trying to maintain a connection, to be responsible for the whole family back in Australia.

KATHIE LEE: It's not uncommon for people to be the caregiver to everybody, is it?

GRANT: Yeah, there was a lot of that. And there was another reason for being drawn to this woman, and it was that she had some very deep beliefs. She'd been reading Scripture for many years. And she followed the Messianic way although she wasn't Jewish.

KATHIE LEE: And that appealed to you?

GRANT: It appealed to me a lot, because you mentioned values and morals, and I hadn't really been connected directly with God over the period of time.

KATHIE LEE: Did you feel like you had lost it or had never had it to lose?

GRANT: No, I was trying to show that my values and the way that I lived my life were, in fact, similar to the values of God that she was talking about.

KATHIE LEE: Did you start going to church with her?

GRANT: No, we never got there. We had a lot of discussions about it. There were some Messianic things that we did, and I chose to be respectful of the things that were important to her. We used to pray together in the first year. And I have to thank her for opening all that up for me.

KATHIE LEE: Okay, so you ultimately broke up. What happened?

GRANT: Yeah, going back, probably about the middle of 2019, things started to change. She said, "I don't want to be with you anymore. I want to get on with my life."

KATHIE LEE: Were you heartbroken?

GRANT: Oh, I can't tell you how heartbroken I was, because it was all my dreams, the future.

KATHIE LEE: So is that when you moved downtown?

GRANT: Yeah, I didn't know where I wanted to live. All I knew was that I wanted to be in the downtown area. I'm used to living downtown in Melbourne, where it's vibrant, where all the options are.

KATHIE LEE: And what was your spiritual condition at the time?

GRANT: Almost from day one of moving in, there was construction going on in the courtyard of the apartments where I was living, and I was stressed. I was just trying to make sense of everything. I'm an athlete, so I started to run again. But the second week of moving into this accommodation, my back went, and I had this extreme pain. And so I had the construction going on, and my back pain, and I was trying to save the business.

KATHIE LEE: And you couldn't return to Australia because of COVID and also because of your immigration status, right?

GRANT: That's right. But then I started to meet people, like Greg and Angie.

KATHIE LEE: The most hospitable, welcoming, godly people. They are the reason I live here too.

GRANT: They just accepted me from day one. They saw me sitting at the coffee shop on my own, and they asked some questions.

KATHIE LEE: Angie tried to set you up with certain people!

GRANT: That's right. And then Greg and Angie just invited me to the next thing and the next thing with a whole bunch of other people.

KATHIE LEE: They made you family, didn't they?

GRANT: They really did, from day one.

KATHIE LEE: Was it obvious to you that their faith was their motivator in life?

GRANT: Well, I saw it very early with them, because I was interested in what their backgrounds were. So that was the beginning of meeting, I guess, people of, let's call it deep faith.

KATHIE LEE: That's what it is.

GRANT: And what was just wonderful is that I didn't feel like I was being judged. There was just this support that appeared out of nowhere.

KATHIE LEE: They weren't prying into your life; they were just there if you needed them?

GRANT: They were just there. And then we had flooding in the apartments. We all had to move out of the apartments, a whole bunch of people who didn't know each other, and we moved into a hotel. Because we couldn't prepare meals and access our apartments, we'd all gather around the bar at the hotel.

KATHIE LEE: Oh, those were great days.

GRANT: It was the most amazing thing because we were sort of all stuck, and it was COVID, so we got to learn about each other. We were asking questions that we'd never had the opportunity to ask. And I discovered they're some of the most amazing people I've ever met in my life. And what was interesting, almost without exception, every person there had faith and belief in God. So it became a great community because we could share our life experiences.

That is where the conversations with Angie and Greg really began, and then, of course, I met you, and you allowed me to be part of your family. It was wonderful. There were all these people who were my supporters. It was just an amazing feeling. I felt safe. I felt part of the community.

KATHIE LEE: You felt loved?

GRANT: I did.

KATHIE LEE: So tell me what happened that night that we prayed?

GRANT: In the lead-up to that, a lot of people had been talking to me and, almost without exception, the conversation was sort of around faith. I started doing my work remotely in a coffee shop because it wasn't great working in the apartment. And people would come up to me and say, "Hey, do you mind if I sit down and have a chat?"

KATHIE LEE: Most people love to talk about themselves.

GRANT: Yeah, and they were opening up, and I was happy for them to talk. And after a while, one of the things I started to put in the conversation was, "What's your relationship with God like? Tell me about that." I was really sort of getting into the deep parts, I guess, of some of the things that troubled them.

KATHIE LEE: Yeah, people are used to "What's your sign?" and all of a sudden it's "What's your relationship with God?" It's a huge leap.

GRANT: Yeah. So this was starting to make more sense to me that "Wow, what I'm doing by just being available and talking to people is really important for them."

KATHIE LEE: And for you.

GRANT: Yeah, I've always wanted to help people. So there were a number of people who would talk quite a bit about God and faith and different Bible verses, and I really felt out of my depth.

KATHIE LEE: Was that embarrassing or frustrating or . . . ?

GRANT: I just would pull back a little bit, you know. I was open to exploring and understanding, but I thought, "*Oh boy, I'm going to have to read the Bible from the front to the back.*"

KATHIE LEE: Feeding your soul.

GRANT: But this one night in the hotel, I was talking to a couple of ladies, and one of them said, "Tell me about your relationship with God." That's what I'd been asking others! At the time, all my friends in the community were all sort of around the bar.

KATHIE LEE: They saw the conversation taking place.

GRANT: Exactly. And then you walked past in the hallway with Greg and Angie, and this lady saw you walking by, and she waved and said, "Come over here—"

KATHIE LEE: Beckoned.

GRANT: And then within minutes, there was a whole bunch of people gathered around me. And you came in and prayed, and it was sort of like a welcome prayer. It was amazing. And I think that's when I finally accepted that this is wonderful.

KATHIE LEE: I led you in the prayer of receiving Jesus, do you remember that? You said you were ready to have Jesus in your life. And I said, "Is that true?" And you said, "Yes." I said, "Well, then, we need to pray."

GRANT: That's right.

KATHIE LEE: And you said, "Okay," and we all got around you. You were on my left, I held your hand, and Angie was on your right?

GRANT: I think she was.

KATHIE LEE: And there were several people all trying to touch you, as I remember. Then you teared up.

GRANT: I did.

KATHIE LEE: But then you said later, when you went back to your room, you did sob. Tell me about that.

GRANT: Yeah, it just, it hit me all at once. I was very emotional during the time, but it was so uplifting. It was just this incredible meaning that was coming into my life. And yes, there were tears, but this calm came over me.

KATHIE LEE: Peace.

GRANT: This peace. And I had the best sleep that I've had. So tears of happiness, I guess, tears of relief and this coming together.

KATHIE LEE: What did you feel besides peace?

GRANT: The word *calm* just keeps coming back. It's like the worry about money, the worry about the business, the worry about everything just seemed to disappear. It almost went straightaway, and my body started to heal as well. I started to get strong again.

KATHIE LEE: That's where a lot of your joy came from, didn't it?

GRANT: That's right. And then there were so many people who got involved with my life.

KATHIE LEE: Building you up.

GRANT: Yeah, because I think they could see that I was open, that I was ready to do it.

KATHIE LEE: You were a new creation.

GRANT: People could see the change in me. And it's just been a wonderful time since then. I started to look at my business in a different way and look at the importance of what I was doing.

KATHIE LEE: Not for the financial gain but as part of God's kingdom, to help people.

GRANT: Yeah, and the money sort of became irrelevant. I can't say it was a calling, but I went, "Wow, this is really important to me."

KATHIE LEE: So when you look back now, do you see the hand of God? There's a scripture, Romans 8:28, that says all things work together for good to those who love God and are called according to His purpose. When you look back at all the painful incidents and how you got here, and everything you had to go through in the relationship, in the business, in the brokenness, do you see the hand of God working in your life every step of the way?

GRANT: Yes, and He was. I didn't know how to access that understanding. It was new to me. A lot of people talk about their moment. For me, it was just like it flowed through me.

KATHIE LEE: Well, when you sit down at the piano, like so many of my friends do, or you sit down with a guitar, that flow that you're talking about is the creativity of the Holy Spirit. All of God's creation sings to the Creator, Jehovah Elohim. And that's why you feel that flowing. You're co-creating with the Creator, and that's what we were born to do. That's why you're so joyful when you do it.

GRANT: The music impact has been significant. I had all these melodies for years. But now if I spend the time, there's a melody every day and lyrics also.

KATHIE LEE: You gave yourself over to it.

GRANT: The music just arrived. I've written twenty good melodies, and I've written lyrics for six. I've also been collaborating with a great friend of mine to write a gospel song that we have titled "Living in the House of God," to be released sometime this year. It's just like, "Wow, this is amazing!"

KATHIE LEE: Like your soul had been dammed up. And once Jesus healed your soul, it flooded with streams of living water.

GRANT: Yeah.

KATHIE LEE: I'm so happy to hear your stories today. Thank you for sharing them.

ELEVEN

YOU ARE NOT ALONE

CHUCK HARMONY AND CLAUDE KELLY (AKA LOUIS YORK)

Since I moved to Tennessee, I often say, "All roads lead to Angie." Because it seems that everyone I've met through my friend and neighbor Angie Clawson has become incredibly meaningful to me.

Two of my absolute favorites are Claude Kelly and Chuck Harmony. Individually, they are among the most successful songwriters and producers in the pop music world. And together, they are the duo known as Louis York because Chuck grew up in East St. Louis and Claude grew up in New York.

I count Chuck and Claude among my most precious treasures. Together, we wrote an oratorio called *The God of the Other Side,* the fourth oratorio in my new project called *The Way*, to be released soon. We have also written many pop songs, but it's our time together just hanging out and sharing life that I value the most.

When they sat down with me at the kitchen table of Angie and her husband, Greg, they might just as well have sat down in my heart and never left. Prepare to fall in love like I did.

KATHIE LEE: You two are my sweet brothers and dear friends. I'm interested in your faith journeys. As I understand, you both grew up with godly moms who really impacted you.

CHUCK: My mom kept me in church for my whole life. I was always going to church: Wednesday night Bible classes, Sunday morning, Sunday afternoon. That was a part of our household: God and religion. My mom to this day is a faithful churchgoer.

CLAUDE: Same. I grew up going to church every Sunday. I grew up Episcopal. My mom's from Jamaica, so a lot of it comes from the Church of England. It was a very structured, cathedral-like church, with liturgical services. But like Chuck, I went every single Sunday, everything in the week, and I sang in the choirs. I was a church kid. Besides school, that was my life.

KATHIE LEE: And would you say the person who's been most impactful in your lives is your mother?

CLAUDE: I'm 100 percent a mama's boy!

CHUCK: I'm 120 percent!

KATHIE LEE: And where were your fathers during this time?

CHUCK: Well, I grew up with my father, but he left when I was about eight. I knew him, but we were never close.

CLAUDE: My father was not a part of my life at all. I just got 200 percent love from my mom. I got so much love from her that I didn't really know I was missing anything.

KATHIE LEE: What do you hear your mother's voice saying to you at this point in your lives?

CHUCK: I used to keep in my wallet a scripture that my mom gave me when I was eight. Philippians 4:13: "I can do all things through Christ who strengthens me."

KATHIE LEE: Somebody told me that the word for "all things" means "for all seasons of your life." Like the verse "To everything there is a season," and the Byrds song, remember that?

CHUCK AND CLAUDE: Yes!

CLAUDE: My mother had this placard on the wall at our apartment in New York City that said, "This too shall pass," and when I moved out, she gave it to me. I always go back to it because it humbles me when things are going good that these things will pass, and when things are bad, I remember that this too shall pass. It's the seasons, the concept of turning over, winter won't last forever, summer won't last forever, and so on.

KATHIE LEE: Chuck, you were married. How long did that marriage last?

CHUCK: Nine months. But we'd been in a five-year relationship, and by the time we got to the altar, we were on shaky ground.

KATHIE LEE: And Claude, you came close.

CLAUDE: I came close. I was in a seven-year relationship. Our moms loved each other. Our families were happy. Chuck liked her. But my relationship ended. It overlapped with what I would call my spiritual awakening. There was nothing devastating that happened. No affair, cheating, or big fight. We just grew apart.

KATHIE LEE: But it's something you'd both welcome? Being in a serious relationship again?

CHUCK AND CLAUDE: Yes!

KATHIE LEE: Boy, does God have a couple of magnificent women waiting for you! But was there a time when you discarded your faith and went down that Hollywood, Grammy-pursuit road? Pursuing your dreams instead of walking in the footsteps of Jesus?

CHUCK: I was always a churchgoer. I felt real condemnation if I didn't go to church on Sunday. That was the programming of my faith. But after a while in the music business, with all the enticing ways, it kind of lured me out of that pattern. There was a point where I felt I was all by myself, with no faith and no real direction.

KATHIE LEE: Did you believe that God was still there?

CHUCK: I've always had too much fear to doubt God. I had a healthy fear, which is respect for God. I kind of doubted what my childhood taught me about faith and religion. I was just drinking a lot and locking myself up in the studio. And it was in that time that I rediscovered my faith.

KATHIE LEE: Praise God because you had a mom praying for you. How long would you say that period lasted?

CHUCK: Right before I moved to New York is when I started to rediscover what my faith meant.

KATHIE LEE: What about you, Claude?

CLAUDE: I actually had a really good church experience growing up. My church was very diverse, and it allowed me to do other things musically. The year I went to college, my church at home fell apart. I wouldn't say I've 100 percent recovered from that. I've spent many years separating my love for God from my lack of faith for the messengers, the teachers.

KATHIE LEE: Remember what Gandhi said, something like, "I would be a Christian, except for all the Christians."

CLAUDE: So it's been a full circle. I've come back around to a stronger faith than I had before because I'm more mature now. And I can separate man-made things from what God is trying to do in my life. It took a lot of removing of resentment and unlearning some of the fantasies and fairy tales that can be damaging to how you actually apply Christianity to your life.

KATHIE LEE: After all your success, everything you've learned, which would you say is more important to you: religion or relationship with a living God?

CHUCK: Relationship. I want to be on the right side of spirituality, and that's relationship.

CLAUDE: For me too. Relationship with God is the core of who I am.

KATHIE LEE: There was a time when you each had enormous success individually. Tell me about what drew you to each other when you finally made that move to say, "We gotta leave LA."

CLAUDE: Well, I was already living in New York. So when Chuck moved from LA to New York, we'd already been working together in the music business for several years. We'd done several hit records for many different labels: Rihanna, Miley Cyrus, Bruno, Janet, Mary J. Blige, Fantasia, Whitney, soundtracks. We were polite associates in business. As soon as a song was done, we'd go home and didn't talk much more.

KATHIE LEE: You were colleagues?

CLAUDE: Yes, a colleague I was always excited to work with. And when Chuck moved to New York, we were around each other more, and we realized that we had the same tastes or didn't tolerate the same things.

KATHIE LEE: Shared values.

CLAUDE: Chuck was new to New York, so I was like, "Let's see New York!" So we rode bikes up and down the Hudson on West Side Highway. And all kinds of stuff.

KATHIE LEE: You started doing life together instead of just making music.

CLAUDE: And we started talking more, and I realized that he was as unhappy on a soul level about what our careers were giving us as I was.

KATHIE LEE: In spite of all the success?

CHUCK AND CLAUDE: Yes.

CLAUDE: I really believe that God put us in each other's lives to be mirrors, because there are a lot of things I wouldn't have manned up about had I not been able to see a mirror of myself. And vice versa.

KATHIE LEE: You really used each other in each other's lives.

CLAUDE: When someone who is brilliant and has a talent that the world needs to hear said to me, "I'm thinking of quitting because I don't feel fulfilled anymore," it sounded crazy that a genius wouldn't want to do what he was born to do. And later, when I told him about my own struggle, he looked at me and said the same thing. Then you can't deny it.

KATHIE LEE: And you realize you're not crazy.

CLAUDE: And you are not alone.

CHUCK: That's the most freeing feeling I've ever felt. I've always felt alone in life, like I have to tread my own path. That's why we named our company the Weirdo Workshop. So our conversation was the first time I could actually see myself in somebody else. And I was like, "Man, I'm not crazy." It was a mutual respect.

KATHIE LEE: That is the sweetest story.

CLAUDE: Some sports are solo sports, and some sports are team sports. And I think the gift I got from our business partnership and friendship was that I had to learn how to run this race together with another human being for it to work. For happiness to be included in the picture.

KATHIE LEE: You, Chuck, were going to do something different?

CHUCK: I was going to go to seminary. I went to the school of preaching when I was twelve, and that side always interested me. I felt like, *"I'm not happy; I don't feel like I'm making a difference in the world or adding positivity to life."*

KATHIE LEE: And I know you felt the same way, Claude. I'm just getting this image of what it's like for you guys sitting down for a writing session like, "Oh, crap. I gotta write another hit song." Was that part of it, the burden of writing hits? I think of, what does it profit a man or woman if they gain the whole world, and they lose their very soul?

CLAUDE: It is a burden any time you're a creative person and you feel caged. Because you're born with a gift, and if that gift can't be fully expressed, it's a burden.

KATHIE LEE: You were using your gifts, but not for the kingdom.

CLAUDE: No. And not truthfully enough. It felt like we were on a constant hamster wheel of doing formulaic music that we knew would make the world feel good enough but not feel complete.

KATHIE LEE: So you made the decision to get back to the roots of your music, your purpose spiritually, and you both had a desire to make your mothers proud.

CLAUDE: Always. Still to this day. We started Louis York, which was formed out of our frustration about the other music we were doing. That led to the company, and we felt New York and LA were too traditional in the music business. So we made a list of cities: Seattle, Denver, Atlanta, Nashville. Once we saw how beautiful Tennessee is, we never looked anywhere else. Sometimes you get a quick revelation. And it was just like, "This is it."

CHUCK: I had been living so far away from my mom. My mom doesn't fly, so she looks at things in driving time. Nashville is like three and a half hours away from her, so she was superexcited.

KATHIE LEE: So you opened up your Weirdo Workshop, and somebody comes knocking at your door. Now, who would that be?

CLAUDE: It was our neighbor Angie, like out of a movie. We were New York hardened and LA jaded. The doors were locked, shades down. There was a knock on the door, and it was Angie with a smile on her face and donuts in her hands, showing Southern hospitality. "Hey, I'm your new neighbor. I saw you all moved in." You can't say no to Angie. There's something so loving and genuine and so forceful . . . in a good way.

KATHIE LEE: She really wants to welcome you!

CLAUDE: You might as well play along because you know you're going to be blessed by whatever adventure she's taking you on. It started a beautiful friendship. Some people are born to be community connectors. And then she said, "Kathie Lee Gifford moved to town, and I want you to meet her." And to be fair, because of our experience in the entertainment industry, we were like, "We didn't move here to get back into the celebrity scene."

KATHIE LEE: I felt the same way, but Angie kept telling me, "You just have to meet them!"

CLAUDE: She said, "Come over to my place, and I'm gonna have you meet Kathie."

KATHIE LEE: It was love at first sight!

CLAUDE: We met a new best friend. We learn from you every time we're around you. Always spiritually, always facts about the Bible, and about the true history and true meaning of things.

KATHIE LEE: You guys had such a hunger for the Word of God.

CLAUDE: You're one of the first people who had facts and geography to back up what you were saying.

CHUCK: And that's why I was going to seminary. I wanted to learn.

KATHIE LEE: Anybody can learn. "Seek My face," God says, "and I'll meet you there."

CLAUDE: I like to be friends with people who can teach me. I consider my closest friends the ones I laugh a lot with, drink good wine with, but also people I'm learning from.

KATHIE LEE: We're living beings, and our souls need to be tended like a garden. Our greater purpose is to share the love of God with people who don't know it yet.

CLAUDE: It really is a community. You said something that really affected us about how the church went underground. When we're together and doing Bible studies, it's the most church I ever feel.

KATHIE LEE: The Christian church didn't have buildings for the first many years. But that's how it thrives. The truth cannot be contained. So when I say the word *Jesus*, what do you think of, Chuck?

CHUCK: *Teacher.* He is the greatest example of humility and power. He's my teacher.

CLAUDE: When I think of Jesus, the first word that comes to my mind also is *Teacher.* He's a teacher.

KATHIE LEE: What do you think is the biggest misconception about Jesus today?

CLAUDE: What scares me is that someone who is universally famous and people model so much after can be so tragically misunderstood in terms of what His teachings are. So much can be done in His name that is the opposite of what He said. This misunderstanding of Jesus is what keeps me in check. The power of your words may last longer than even your life.

CHUCK: That's for sure.

CLAUDE: I'm also wary of myself, how I ingest information. The Jesus I've learned to know is much better than the version they gave me as a kid. I'm alarmed every day when I see online how misunderstood He is. And the lessons are not complicated. They're pretty simple.

KATHIE LEE: Well, two thousand years ago, they crucified Him for these very things. They knew the scripture in Isaiah that this Messiah would be a humble, suffering servant, and He was fulfilling prophecy all over the place, but they were blinded to it. So if they were blinded to it when He was among them doing the most amazing miracles, how much harder is it now to get His message across? That's why we, as His disciples, need to put that example before every decision we make. That old saying, "What would Jesus do?"

CLAUDE: It's cliché, but it's accurate.

KATHIE LEE: He would love.

CHUCK: I don't think we are in tune with what Jesus would do.

KATHIE LEE: I think the greatest Christians who ever lived battled with it. What Jesus did was not human nature. Turn the other cheek? Give him your cloak even though you'll freeze to death? Lay down your life for your friends? But we're human.

CLAUDE: The word *discipleship* is a thing that's gotten me to a better place with God. We are walking disciples today. Our community here is disciples. Not because we're studying but because it's happening now.

KATHIE LEE: It's humbling, isn't it? He's the same yesterday, today, and forever.

CLAUDE: The same miracles are happening today.

KATHIE LEE: What are you most looking forward to in your life?

CHUCK: I'm looking forward to growing in truth. Now that I've found the nucleus of my faith and what my life should be, I want to grow in that. That's what I want my life to be.

CLAUDE: I want to spread this feeling, this joy, this music, this community with as many people who are willing to open up and try something different. It feels criminal to be this creative and happy and inspired and keep that antidote to yourself.

KATHIE LEE: Yes, because we have the cure for the malignancy of the soul.

CLAUDE: I want to show it. I want to live it. I want people to see it when we're onstage or when we're out together. I want people to see us and think, "*There's something different about those people. I want that medicine.*"

TWELVE

COURAGE WITH CONVICTIONS

JANICE DEAN

For longtime viewers of Fox News Channel, Janice Dean is a familiar, enduring, and delightful fixture. Even when she's covering the bad weather happening in different areas of the country, she is a consistently sunny fixture. I became friendly with Janice when she was writing her first children's book, featuring a lovable frog named Freddy, who's fascinated by all things weather. It was published with great success, and Janice went on to write five more books. I was always pleased to support her efforts with an endorsement or a foreword.

I have watched and admired Janice's courage and her convictions this past year as she battled for justice for her beloved in-laws after losing them to COVID-19 in New York. Here is her story in her own words.

KATHIE LEE: Janice, I've known you for several years now and admired you and your darling books with Freddy the weather frog. Tell me, what kind of a home did you grow up in? What was your childhood like?

JANICE: It was a good childhood. When I look back on it, my mom and dad were together for many years. They were divorced when I was in my twenties. I didn't see my dad a whole lot. He was what you'd call a workaholic. He loved what he was doing. One of the biggest pieces of advice he gave me was find something you love to do, and it will never feel like work.

KATHIE LEE: That's what my dad said to me!

JANICE: He really took that to heart because we never really saw him that much. He worked all the time. He really loved what he did. He helped with politics, and he was also a systems engineer. He was a very smart man. I think we had one of the first computers that were available. He knew one day we'd be on the internet looking for information.

We were brought up Catholic. We went to church. Dad was an altar boy growing up. My mom was also Catholic. So we were brought up in the tradition of church, Sunday school, holidays. I also remember my dad went bankrupt several times. He worked so hard, but he was also someone who liked to invest in things that were very chancy. We moved many times because all of sudden we would have a lot of money, and then he'd blow it all. We moved to different neighborhoods, from a big house to a smaller house in a different neighborhood. I remember my mom being sad sometimes. And I remember when he said he no longer believed in God, so we stopped going to church. Looking back on that, he thought a lot of his troubles were because God didn't love him or that God had failed him somehow.

But I still wanted faith in my life as a young girl. My best friend's mom was in a choir at a United church. At the time, I didn't really know the different religions, but I loved her voice, so I would go to church with her and sing in the choir with her. Her mom was the choir director. And then I joined a youth group with the church and really loved that and wanted to be part of that.

KATHIE LEE: You had community there. It's called fellowship.

JANICE: Of course! Even though my father had decided religion was not going to be a part of his life, I still wanted it in my life and followed it through the eyes of my girlfriend and her family.

KATHIE LEE: When you say United Church, do you mean a unity church?

JANICE: The United Church of Canada is Protestant. It's the largest Protestant Christian denomination in Canada.

KATHIE LEE: Was your mother upset with you? Did she continue to go to a Catholic church?

JANICE: She wasn't upset. She was actually the one who brought me to Sunday school early on. I think she wanted me to feel faith in my life. Later on she kind of followed along with what my father was doing. Church was no longer a part of their lives, but I still wanted it. I found the community, the youth group. I remember having a crush on one of the youth group leaders! We had dances and so forth. I never thought of it as a religious group, just a lot of friends getting together.

So fast-forward to when I met my husband, who was also Catholic, went to Catholic school, grew up in a Catholic family. My niece is a Catholic schoolteacher.

Sean and I actually got married at city hall. We got married later in life. I was thirty-seven; he was thirty-eight. We never really went to church, but we both had faith and believed in God.

But ten years later, Sean said, "Let's get married in church, in front of a priest." So we went to the church, Holy Trinity, where Father Gary was a good friend. He met with us. We said we wanted to get married in a church and make it official. He said, "Why not make it the whole thing? A real wedding!" It was beautiful. We had very close friends there. We got married in front of friends and family, and our boys were there. I bought a dress at Lord & Taylor, and Sean bought a suit. Megyn Kelly was my maid of honor, and Shannon Bream did a reading. And church has been a part of our life since then. Our son goes to Catholic school, and I love reading with him and learning about all the things I learned about as a child and having it all come back.

KATHIE LEE: That is beautiful! What was your first impression of Jesus when you were growing up?

JANICE: Well, the visual of Him is on the cross, right? How He gave it all for all of us. And I also remember when I went to Sunday school obviously at Christmastime, Mary and Jesus and the animals and the wise men. So those are certainly fond memories. I do remember being a little afraid of Jesus on the cross as a young child. And now, I see my youngest child going through that as well, you know, what He did for us. Theodore, my son, has recently said, "Mom, what is sinning? What is sin?" So listening to him and his worries, I know that I was worrying about that, too, as a child and thinking, "*I don't want to disappoint God.*"

KATHIE LEE: So you totally believed in Jesus as a historical figure?

JANICE: Yes.

KATHIE LEE: Did you have a religion or a relationship or both? Like a religion, following the rules, or a relationship, following in His footsteps and His teachings every day? Have you had a relationship with the living God your whole life?

JANICE: I think so. I don't think of it every day. Certainly we pray every day as a family, especially my youngest, who likes to pray every night, so I pray with him.

I always knew there was a higher power. People say to me, "How did you have the courage to move from Canada to New York City with just a suitcase and no money and believe in yourself?" I have to believe that I was giving myself to a higher power and that God was going to take care of me, and whatever was going to happen to me was predestined. That kind of faith comes from believing that the path that I'm meant to go down is in front of me. I don't quite know where it leads, but I have faith in God and faith in a higher power that it will lead me to what my destination is going to be.

KATHIE LEE: But you never dreamed that it would ultimately lead you to the kind of year you just experienced! Please take us back. When did your in-laws go into the nursing home?

JANICE: I'm glad you asked me that, because that is one of the hardest decisions that families have to go through. People are very quick to judge: "Why did they put their parents in a home? Why didn't they just take care of them themselves?" And you have to really sit down and find out what their reasonings were and why they made their decisions.

So my in-laws lived in a four-story walk-up in Brooklyn for over fifty years. It was their home. For many years, my husband and his sister would say to them, "We have to get you out of this apartment. There's gonna be a day when you're not going to be able to get down these stairs. We'll help you find a place that has easy access." They always said, "No, we don't want to do that. We're just going to continue living here." And it got to a point where his dad's health was failing. Mickey, his dad, was in his mideighties, and he had early-stage dementia. That got worse. His mom, Dee, was taking care of him, but she was having back problems. We had aides visiting them, but it got to the point where his parents couldn't take care of each other.

So Sean took his mom to several assisted-living residences that were close to us on Long Island. She found a wonderful one that had a double room so Mickey could join after he left his rehab facility. It was a tough time, but the goal was that they were going to be close to us in this place. That's what we thought would be the best option for them. We made that decision because we loved them, and we wanted to make sure they were taken care of.

Not long after this happened, COVID-19 took over. In March, everyone was quarantined in New York, especially his dad at rehab. We were getting reports from his nursing home on a fairly regular basis. One Saturday, we got a call saying, "Your father-in-law isn't feeling well. He's running a fever." I said, "Okay, please give me an update." Three hours later, we got a call that he was dead! We weren't able to see him or talk to him. I pray that there was a kind person with him when he took his last breath.

KATHIE LEE: Was Dee with him?

JANICE: No, she was in the assisted-living place, waiting for him. My husband had to call his mom to tell her. There's no word to describe what that was like for Dee. Sean and I had discussions about bringing Dee to our house, but we were advised against that because it would present more of an issue.

Sean was able to see his mom once. He delivered her some orchids and cards and photos of the kids and Mickey. He had to be six feet away and wearing a mask and didn't get to hug her. He told her, "Mom, please just hang on." But she got sick and died a few days later. We weren't able to see them or comfort them. We weren't able to have funerals for them. My sister-in-law was friends with a funeral director in Staten Island, and he said, "I will bury your parents." I tell my sons they were buried together, and they are together in heaven.

KATHIE LEE: So where was Jesus for you, Janice, during this terrible year?

JANICE: Well, I prayed a lot. I prayed for strength. I prayed for strength for my husband. And I felt closer to God. Our church in our neighborhood was so wonderful. They reached out asking what they could do to help. And there were churches all over the country who said they would honor my in-laws in their services. People sent me beautiful prayer cards. I felt love and prayers, and working at Fox News Channel, I just knew that the audience was praying for our family. I never felt closer to God at that time because I felt like I was leaning on Him.

KATHIE LEE: You are a beautiful example of godliness. I've watched you, and I want you to know how incredibly proud I am of you. And the times I've prayed for you during this painful year, I'm sure I was among thousands of people saying, "Lord, give this beautiful lady courage." God has used you in a powerful way. The peace of Christ I pray over you.

JANICE: The one thing I think of every day is the psalm "The Lord is near to the brokenhearted and saves the crushed in spirit." That has saved me.

THIRTEEN

TAKING JESUS TO THE METAL MAINSTREAM

BRIAN WELCH

People are always stunned to learn that I am very good friends with the dreadlocked, full-body-tattooed lead guitarist of the heavy metal band Korn. I just laugh and answer, "Why wouldn't I be?"

Brian "Head" Welch is the sweetest and most tenderhearted man. His story is the stuff of legend. A few years ago, Brian released a very raw documentary called *Loud Krazy Love*, which received rave reviews. We sat down to discuss his life for I Am Second, an organization of which my dear friend, Angie Clawson, is the heart and soul.

~

KATHIE LEE: We're a bit of an odd couple! Many people have watched your movie. Of those three words—*loud, crazy, love*—which is most truthful about you?

BRIAN: *Love*. Some would say *loud*, and some would say *crazy*, but the true essence is love, because Christ is love.

KATHIE LEE: But you didn't know that for a long time, did you?

BRIAN: No.

KATHIE LEE: Some of the early scenes in your movie are about how crazy it was. Knowing you the way I know you now, I see you as the calm Brian, a man who's at peace with yourself. But I didn't know you in those days. How hard was it for you to be that raw in your movie?

BRIAN: I think I was given grace, which to me is the empowerment to live the life that Christ wants us to live. Because we can't do anything on our own strength.

KATHIE LEE: Not a thing.

BRIAN: I felt like this generation needs real, raw, authentic. I just put it all out there. I was so sick of living a lie, a depressed, empty, lonely life. I was just like the blind guy in the Bible, who was like, "I don't know anything about anything, but I was blind and now I can see because of this guy." That was what happened to me. I was a loser, an addict, and now I'm fixed.

KATHIE LEE: Well, a little baby came into your life.

BRIAN: Yea. Jennea.

KATHIE LEE: Beautiful girl. Your life had become so muddied, so dirty and impure—and all of a sudden, you were holding this perfect creature. Tell me about that moment.

BRIAN: Well, there's nothing like being able to hold a miracle you create. And so just seeing her come into the world, it was like a healing balm into my soul. Realizing, "Wow, it's so much more than me." And little did I know that it's much more than me and her. There's this great big God who loves me and you more than we love our kids. And it all comes from Him and flows through us. Yeah, Jennea was like an angel sent from God to get me to wake up. Now, you have two kids. Same for you, right?

KATHIE LEE: Totally. But I didn't come from the world that you came from.

BRIAN: You weren't killing yourself with drugs and alcohol?

KATHIE LEE: Actually, it was sex addiction. Ha ha ha. No, I was Miss Goody Two-shoes. But I needed Christ, and I needed redemption, and I needed healing every bit as much as the so-called worst sinners. We're all sinners, and we're all saved by grace. That's the beauty of the cross. What was the reaction from your fans when you left Korn and announced that you'd found Jesus? Were people mad at you that you were no longer that guy?

BRIAN: There was a mixture of reactions, but most people thought I had just done one too many lines.

KATHIE LEE: They thought you were crazier than ever?

BRIAN: Yeah, like, "He thinks he's talking to Jesus." But they don't understand the beauty of the spiritual world where Christ, actually—instead of hearing the words—you feel the love and the communication through the love and the peace. At first, I was cursed with thinking, "*I gotta get another line, another sack of drugs*," and then when I met Christ, it was like, "*You're never gonna be the same. You're gonna be the best dad.*" And I was cursed with positive thoughts. It was amazing.

KATHIE LEE: And then you gave up everything because you thought that's what Jesus wanted you to do. I love that people encouraged you to go back to the world you came out of and see that as your true mission field. Just this afternoon, my makeup artist said, "Oh, you're interviewing Brian Welch this afternoon. My husband was Korn's biggest fan, and he came to know Christ through Brian's testimony."

BRIAN: And that's a sign right there of what it's all about. We just share our Christ's love with the people we're called to be in relationship with. Whether it's you on the *Today* show and Christ's love is coming out of you to your followers, or if it's a fan-musician thing, and Christ's love is coming out of me to my followers, it's amazing to see what He is doing.

When I grew up, I didn't see too much about God in the mainstream. But God is moving in a new way in our generation. It's amazing to see. It's like we are saying to people, "Look, we're different, but we have the same heart." Jesus called some of the religious people "whitewashed tombs" because they looked good on the outside but didn't have the heart inside.

KATHIE LEE: Yes, inside they were dead men's bones. The word for *hypocrite* means "actor." That's when you don't have any true relationship with a living God. You're acting out a part, and isn't that so many of us on the world's stage? We're acting.

BRIAN: I love coming to your house because you give me these nuggets that you learn from the Rabbi.

KATHIE LEE: What was the hardest scene to keep in the movie for you?

BRIAN: Talking about the porn stuff, because my mom's gonna watch it. I mean, that's just life because a lot of guys struggle with pornography. But one of the hardest things for me to watch in the movie was my daughter in the swim meet, where she's winning the race. I remember that time so vividly. I think I'd done Vicodin before the meth, and I was so broken that she was achieving all this stuff and I wasn't there. God was using that empty hole and depression to get me to look elsewhere besides the crazy rock-star life.

KATHIE LEE: What I saw as I was watching the movie was that you started to love somebody more than you loved yourself. Real *agape* love. Unconditional, like God's love for us. You were starting to sense what that was about, and, wow, it's mind-blowing like no drug can be.

BRIAN: Yep. And you get instantly addicted once you get your eyes open to that. You start to know it's real, and you start to believe it. It's not blind faith, though. It's like an interaction, relationship based, heart to heart, spirit to spirit. Really amazing.

KATHIE LEE: When you're holding your child, she just sees love from you. She doesn't care about your Grammys, your bank account, your trophies. She just sees her daddy. You didn't want to let her down. It's the thought that you would not be there for her. Your parents were great parents; they came off as rock stars in this movie. How great and loving and supportive they were! I can't imagine how worried they were about you.

BRIAN: My mom said I hid it really well. I'd say, "I'm just tired from the road." Meanwhile, I was eating Vicodin like Tic Tacs. Doing lines. But that was when I was traveling. When I came home, I'd taper down.

KATHIE LEE: You knew how to clean up when you had to. I want to talk to you about the writing now. Many artists come back, and they don't have that same hard-edged thing in their music anymore because they've been cleaned up and they're new creations in Christ. But my makeup artist's husband, who came to Christ because of your testimony, said you've been doing work with Korn that is beyond any of the early stuff he was insane about, especially *The Serenity of Suffering*. That had to be a challenge to record. You were sitting down with your bandmates again, and everybody knew what had happened with you. You weren't going to be glorifying that life anymore. You're a new person. How do you as an artist sit there with your guys and go, "What are we going to write about now?"

BRIAN: I think it's just everyone in the group got older. We're all in our fifties now. It's like you grow up, you know. Sometimes you add the pain. Some songs are just fun and good times. I don't think God is sitting there and taking notes. Mainly our singer's been singing about pain and anger. I love the new stuff. He's grieving the loss of his wife. Whether they know it or not, and I think they do, God is working through them with all of this stuff.

KATHIE LEE: So how is Jennea doing now?

BRIAN: She's awesome. You saw her on her twenty-first birthday. She's working at the boarding school where she was in the film. She went through the school, and now she's on staff there, mentoring kids. I've always wanted her to be unique and have a heart to help people. And she's getting paid for it.

KATHIE LEE: What's gonna happen when she brings a guy home?

BRIAN: I'll get a couple of Korn security guys, and we're gonna grill him. No, I'm ready. I just want the best for her.

KATHIE LEE: What about you, your heart? Do you think you'll have a love in your life again?

BRIAN: Yeah, I do, and I have for sixteen years now. I have Christ Jesus.

KATHIE LEE: You know what I mean.

BRIAN: Yeah, no, I don't know. Maybe one day. I'm not looking.

KATHIE LEE: Well, love finds you. You don't find love; love finds you.

BRIAN: Is that a Korn song?

KATHIE LEE: That's a Kathie Lee song—they're often confused! Because of your image, people assume things about you, and they couldn't be more wrong when they get to know you.

BRIAN: Yeah, you judge on the outside sometimes. We go to that, and we have to train ourselves to get away from it. I do that with other people sometimes.

KATHIE LEE: What do you think is the biggest misconception about you?

BRIAN: That I'm rough and rugged and scary. I remember coming back from a trip to Australia. Everyone on the plane was silent and reading, and I heard a little kid say, "Mommy, that's a bad man." Everyone looked at me. That's a misconception. Everyone went back to reading, and I looked at him and growled. Ha ha. It was just for fun.

KATHIE LEE: What's the one thing you have to work on in your own life right now?

BRIAN: Maybe worry.

KATHIE LEE: Oh, really? What do you worry about?

BRIAN: The unknown. Well, look at the world.

KATHIE LEE: Yeah. It's hard, but our sovereign God is still on the throne.

BRIAN: Things have to get better, because things are not doing too good right now.

KATHIE LEE: Do you think Jesus is coming back pretty soon?

BRIAN: I don't know about all that. I think every generation since Jesus walked the earth has gotten it wrong. I don't want to repeat past mistakes. I want to learn.

KATHIE LEE: So with the wisdom you have now and the Holy Spirit guiding you, what would you say to a young kid, like you were, who thinks music is the way he should go with his life? Is it worth it?

BRIAN: I think that people are given gifts in this world. Art and music are great gifts to carry, but you need to realize your identity first. If your identity is wrapped up in that, then you'll come crashing down because there are so many ups and downs in life. If you find out who you are in God, and God is in you, then you'll save yourself so much heartache, crashing and burning. I know we all have to go on our own path. You grew up right, and you did the right things, but you still got off the path. We all will. But I think if you have the right foundation, which is relationship with God and identity about who you are, then you have a lot better chance not to crash as hard.

KATHIE LEE: If you were going to write one last song, what would you write about?

BRIAN: It would just be a thank-you song of gratitude for my life and for everything that God has done in my life. It would be *thank you*. One hundred percent. What about you?

KATHIE LEE: The same. So grateful for the Lord and all He has done for me. I love you, brother.

BRIAN: I love you too.

FOURTEEN

GOD LISTENS TO OUR PRAYERS

BRENDA SCHOENFELD

My precious friend Brenda Schoenfeld is one of the most beautiful, gifted, and loving individuals I have ever known. Her heart is as open and tender as you will ever experience, yet her life experiences would suggest that she would have lost her sense of innocence long ago.

I just say her name, and I smile with a million memories. Let's take a trip to the iconic Hotel du Cap-Eden-Roc in Cap d'Antibes, South of France, when our kids were little, and meet Brenda and her adorable son, Diego.

KATHIE LEE: I pray for you every day, and I've loved you forever. Could we go back to that time when we met at the Hotel du Cap? It was summertime. Frank and I saw you everywhere we went, with your son and his scooter. You were always so friendly to everybody. I remember Frank and I saying, "She's either royalty of some sort, or she is the highest-class hooker we have ever seen!"

BRENDA: I do remember that, my Kathie. I do.

KATHIE LEE: Tell me, even though you looked like a woman who had it all together and were obviously a terrific mother, what was going on in your life emotionally?

BRENDA: Oh, Kathie, it was a very difficult time for me. I was having to make terms with the fact that my husband was no longer going to be my husband. And I had a child to raise. And I was thinking of the path I must take now to guide him to beautiful choices that I pray for. So it was a very, very difficult time even though, like you said, it didn't appear so. Nights of worrying, "*How am I going to do this?*"

KATHIE LEE: Tell me what had happened in your marriage to get you to this point.

BRENDA: Well, my husband was having an affair, which he confessed to me. You know, marriages go through ups and downs, but that was a lot to stomach. I was angry. I was sad. You know, just a lot of emotions. Mainly, I think the hardest thing was that I had to keep my feelings inside and try to be a steady human being, mother, everything to my son. That was the hardest part for me.

KATHIE LEE: That's so hard, sweetie. How much did Diego at that young age know of your pain, do you think?

BRENDA: I think children are intuitive. I think he was feeling it, carrying some of my sadness as well, and that really worried me.

KATHIE LEE: Yes. Little people don't deserve big-people problems.

BRENDA: Yes.

KATHIE LEE: Did your husband marry the woman with whom he was having the affair?

BRENDA: No, he did not. Apparently they went on for a little bit, but it eventually ended.

KATHIE LEE: But the damage was done. Did you and your husband try to save your marriage?

BRENDA: Yes, we did. We both tried to work it out, Kathie, but the damage was very severe. It was just difficult, and I don't think we really got past that.

KATHIE LEE: Now, you've always had faith in God, right? Did you grow up in the Catholic Church?

BRENDA: We grew up in a Catholic town and went to a Catholic church. I would say that I had a lot of faith, but I didn't really have a religion.

KATHIE LEE: Tell me, to what extent did you rely on that faith, the God you knew then? What did God look like to you back then?

BRENDA: Well, for some reason, I've always known that God was love. There were things that were magical about that institution, the Catholic church that I grew up in, like when the bells rang and it was time for prayer. I, in silence, went into my own prayer. It was nice.

KATHIE LEE: What would a prayer from you have sounded like at that time?

BRENDA: Well, I remember just saying, "*God, I know Your light, and I know Your love. Please stay close to me. Show me ways to be a good girl, to be a good person.*" For some reason, the first thing I can remember about God when I was a little girl was going through my own journey of unification with Him. I have been very creative since I was a little girl. Every time I did something, I felt like, you know, I was doing it for Him.

KATHIE LEE: Right, because you're an artist. And since we're created in God's image, then we are creators too. And that's why you're so joyful in the work that you do. You bring beauty into the world in everything you do. Any time you design a piece of jewelry or your homes, it's a magnificent expression, I feel, of God's tranquility and serenity and innate beauty. More than almost anyone I've ever known.

BRENDA: I think that's a beautiful thing to say. Any time that I've been in great despair or doubt or even anger, sometimes I just go into this quiet place and I feel at peace. I feel serenity, and, you know, I feel calmer. I always feel like, "*Ah, God, there You are.*"

KATHIE LEE: Well, as bad as this time was in your life, and God did get you through it, there was a very harrowing episode in your life years before in Taxco, Mexico. Do you want to share that part of your story?

BRENDA: Yes, well, I was kidnapped as a young girl.

KATHIE LEE: How old were you?

BRENDA: I was about sixteen. There was an older man than me. Probably twenty-eight or twenty-nine. He kidnapped me and kept me away for three nights. They were the longest days of my life. I was abused, and it was a very difficult time for me. I kept on praying and praying. It was a horrible thing. I guess it can turn a person bitter or angry. For some reason—*thank You, Lord*—it did not. I guess I have found forgiveness. It did make me grow up a lot faster, though, for sure.

KATHIE LEE: Your family was looking for you then. Did they have to pay a ransom for you?

BRENDA: No, the man was the son of a very powerful official. Unfortunately, he got very violent, and he pulled out a gun and shot himself. He did not die. But that was pretty traumatic.

KATHIE LEE: He did that in front of you?

BRENDA: Yes, and in my lap I had blood, and I was screaming. And the bodyguards were like, "Now we're gonna rape you and kill you." All I could think about is, "*I'm gonna die.*" It was horrible, but I kept on praying and praying. We got to the hospital, and at that moment I ran out of the car and yelled, "Help me! Help me!"

The story continued, believe it or not. Even though my family sent me to America to be safe, one time I wanted to surprise my parents, so I went to Mexico. And our town was far away, so I stayed in a hotel. I walked out to the street to get some tacos, and there he was. He kidnapped me again, and he took me to a motel and started beating me. I thought, "*I'm going to die*" again.

KATHIE LEE: So there was never any justice for you?

BRENDA: No, you see, when you have that much power, you can do anything. It was horrible, but to end the story, I heard later through the grapevine that he was killed. So that was the end of that.

KATHIE LEE: So your beautiful story is also full of pain. Nobody would know that from looking at you. How did that experience change your relationship toward men or toward God?

BRENDA: When I first met my husband, we were in love. It was a Cinderella story, really. He was a very affluent man. We were traveling, and we had everything. But the birth of my son, I mean, it was like the most beautiful thing I have ever experienced. I think that changed me because I knew that, more than ever, I could never let anything of my past be passed on.

KATHIE LEE: Yes, if it was resonant in you, it could be passed on to your child.

BRENDA: Yes, and so, fast-forward, my mother died of pancreatic cancer at fifty-eight. It was horrible. My mother said to me at the last breakfast we had, "*Mi hija*, my daughter, do you know what cancer is?" I looked at her straight in her eyes. She said, "Cancer is resentment, hate, unlove for others," and she went on and on in all these negatives. She said, "You must promise me that you will never hold hate, despair, or anger in your heart. Any time you feel that, you pray, 'God, You come in here right now. Right this second.' And in that moment, you have a conversation with God about it. And you and Him clear it up. He will speak to you, and it will be gone."

That was really incredible. All these things go back to the puzzle that is the journey of my life as of today, this beautiful day, at this particular hour that I am alive. Thank You, God. I'm grateful.

KATHIE LEE: Oh, that's so powerful, sweetie. So the years went by after your marriage ended, you dated different people, and there was disappointment. But you were still hopeful that God would bring a beautiful love to you. I want to get back to that day when we were on the deck on Nantucket. That's the day Frank and I almost died in a plane crash. And I remember thinking, "*Brenda's going to be waiting for us, so we can't die in a plane crash.*" I don't remember exactly how long before we ended up talking on my terrace. What do you remember from that conversation?

BRENDA: Oh, I do remember! I was not a Christian then. I do recall that you were speaking, and you held my hand and started to pray. For the longest time, every single time you prayed with me, Kathie, it was as if I was getting one step closer to knowing something bigger and more beautiful. Every time, one more step.

KATHIE LEE: Like a painting that fills in.

BRENDA: Yes, yes, yes. Beautiful.

KATHIE LEE: And then I just asked you, as I often do with anyone I sense is ready to receive the fullness of God into their heart, I said, "Brenda, are you ready to ask Jesus into your heart?" You said, "Yes, please." It was so simple and so sweet. I was as happy as you were. Tell me what changed in your life at that moment. He had a name then, didn't He?

BRENDA: Yes, Jesus.

KATHIE LEE: Tell me what happened on that trip to Israel we took together, when you saw where He walked.

BRENDA: First of all, it was the most pivotal moment. I had no real knowledge of Jesus. In Israel, it became an opportunity to know what my faith really meant. And I knew this was one way to get to know Jesus. I was in the front of the bus, because I get nauseous. You kindly would always be there with me. It was one more sign from God that "*I have your back. I'm here with you, walking in this path.*"

I had been this little girl thinking God is love, but then I'm like all of a sudden, "Jesus is love." God, the Holy Spirit, and the Son. It was the answer I'd been waiting for my whole life. It would heal all the wrong passages that I had taken.

That trip to Israel was Jesus and God and this whole embrace of love. I started collecting rocks in every place. I made a little cross. I wanted to make sure to use every one of those rocks I collected. I'd never read the Bible. And it was like, little by little, collecting these rocks, God saying, "*Everything will be okay, and you will learn about My Word. You will learn.*" I am terribly dyslexic. I cannot read very well. It scared me, but every day it was more and more beautiful.

And then I got baptized in the Jordan River. I spoke to God first to let Him know that I was making that commitment. I prayed, "*I don't know the Bible, but that doesn't make me not Your child. Because You said that I am made in Your image, and I am loved.*" It was my own relationship with Him.

KATHIE LEE: Everybody came from a different place. That was my favorite trip ever. I said, "Lord, You lead each person to this place. You show me who should be there." Every single one had some sort of a life-transforming encounter with Jesus in the Holy Land.

BRENDA: You recount it so beautifully.

KATHIE LEE: Let's go forward now to your life in Texas. Where did you meet Gip?

BRENDA: I met Gip on the "bubble thing"—that is what I called it.

KATHIE LEE: The Bumble dating app?

BRENDA: Yes. I prayed so much. And I want you to know that for two years after Israel, I didn't want to see men. I wanted to be clean, really ready for a new relationship. And ever since Israel, I started writing down everything that I desired in a relationship. Everything in a man, in another soul I would love and take into my life. He must be close to Jesus, he must love his children, he must be a good father. Even to the point that I wanted him to have wrinkles in the left and the right eye. The finest details. When I read some of these things now, it's like, "Wow."

In Israel when I was at the wall, I prayed, "*I am leaving here, and I'm going now back to my world over there. I'm telling You, Papa, here is everything that I need and desire because I know that is the person You are going to send for me.*" I wrote it down, and I said to God, "Here is the text of all the things I ask." And guess what? "Ask, and it shall be given." I asked from my heart and my soul, and what I asked was something pure and good. Then I met him. We had one date, and that was it.

KATHIE LEE: Look at God's faithfulness, Brenda.

BRENDA: I'm telling you, darling. I think all of us, when we really ask from our hearts and from the deepness of our souls, it will come. It will come to you because God does listen.

KATHIE LEE: And He does want to give us the desires of our hearts. He loves His children with an all-consuming fire of a love. He withholds no good and perfect gift from us. And once we start understanding that goodness of God's heart, we start to expect those blessings. Because He's promised us.

BRENDA: Well, I see it. And in conclusion, I have a relationship, a vivid relationship with Jesus. And it connects to everything. It guides my life every day in everything I do. Everything I do, I do it for Him.

KATHIE LEE: Brenda, I knew you had to be in this book. This is beautiful.

FIFTEEN

MESSENGER OF THE MESSIAH

RABBI JASON SOBEL

I first met Rabbi Jason Sobel at Christmastime in Manhattan—my least favorite time of year in New York City. While it may be a thrill for tourists to celebrate the season in Manhattan, it was a furious, frenzied, and frantic time for those of us who actually made a living at Rockefeller Center. Add in the spiritual emptiness of a secular celebration, and it was a recipe for despair.

The only "reason for the season" was blatantly clear: commerce. And it saddened me that the Jesus I knew and loved—the Messiah prophesied through the centuries to save humankind from sin—was nowhere to be found, and definitely not worshiped.

Into this atmosphere the rabbi entered into my cynical malaise. He explained, meticulously and profoundly, the actual biblical account of the Messiah's birth. You can read about it in its entirety in our book *The Rock, the Road, and the Rabbi.*

Since that life-transforming day, Rabbi Jason has continued to illuminate the truth of the Scriptures to me and kept the fire of faith blazing in my heart. I was thrilled to have him share his own personal story of radical transformation through coming to faith in the Messiah, Jesus—also known by His Hebrew name, *Yeshua*.

KATHIE LEE: Let's hear your story of how God began to move you when you were younger.

RABBI JASON: Being Jewish was extremely important to the Sobel household. After all, our family was a living legacy of Holocaust survivors. Most of my mom's relatives died during the Holocaust, so being Jewish was always something deeply ingrained in the very fibers of my being. I grew up with a rich understanding of my identity as a Jew. I prepared for my bar mitzvah at the age of thirteen and attended synagogue every Saturday morning, learning to read Hebrew and the traditional Jewish prayers. But my passion became basketball and music. When I entered high school, the basketball coach said, "If you don't play football, I'm going to bench you for basketball." I didn't want to play football. There were three things that nice Jewish boys didn't do: no tattoos, no motorcycles, and no football.

KATHIE LEE: Well, that's in the Torah, right? Ha ha.

RABBI JASON: Well, I didn't play football, and sure enough, the coach benched me. One day, he was dogging me out, and I got fed up and threw a basketball at his head. That ended my basketball career! Then, in the infinite wisdom of my youth, I wound up hanging out with the high school DJ and drug dealer. I dropped out of high school, partying with a rough crowd in New York City and getting into trouble. I became a DJ and eventually found myself working in a large music recording studio in New York City, where many famous rock and rap stars recorded. They had fame and fortune, everything I thought I wanted. But when I looked at their lives, it was very clear they were not happy. They were doing drugs in front of their kids and all sorts of other craziness. I realized, "*There has to be more to life.*" That was when I began my spiritual journey. I began studying and reading Eastern philosophy and religion. Through the process of unanswered questions leading to more questions, I became a "Jew-Bu," a New Age Jew. I was looking for meaning and purpose. I had a hunger and a thirst for the divine and spiritual power in my life. I was willing to travel to the ends of the earth to discover answers to my questions: Is there a God? For what purpose am I created? Is there more in life than fame and fortune?

KATHIE LEE: How old were you?

RABBI JASON: I was about eighteen. I began to study yoga, and I wanted to become a doctor of Oriental medicine. I got into meditation, yoga, and martial arts, but I was also studying with my rabbi at the synagogue. I was looking for a genuine encounter with God. I became a vegetarian and took a vow of poverty. I wanted to go to India to study with a guru.

One day, I was meditating, and my soul began to vibrate, and it left my body. This may sound dramatic, but this experience was authentic. My spirit began to lift out of my body, and it went through the roof and through the clouds into heaven. The next thing I knew, I saw this King, high and lifted up on a throne surrounded by glorious light. I felt His love and His power pulsating through every cell in my body. I came alive in a way I had never experienced before. Every cell in my being could feel God and His love. I felt completely connected and at peace in this state of euphoria. The King began to speak to me, and I knew the King on the throne was Yeshua-Jesus, and He said, "*Many are called, but few are chosen.*" I said, "Lord, am I chosen?" He sweetly replied, "*Yes.*" I was overwhelmed and didn't want to leave. He told me I had to go back home.

You may be asking, How could a nice Jewish boy from Jersey know who Jesus was? Honestly, there was just something deep inside of me that just knew. To this date, it was the best experience of my life. The encounter was unmatchable in every way and the experience of a lifetime.

I was instantly back down in my room, shaking under the power of His presence but with a complete sense of shalom, peace, and joy. I was running around outside saying, "I'm called to serve Him!" Just at this moment, my mom pulled up into the driveway, and she saw her good little Jewish son running around in circles, like a crazy man, in her front yard for all the neighbors to gawk at. Surely, she thought I was *mashugana*—a Yiddish term describing a person who is nonsensical, silly, or crazy. I didn't care, as I was so elated, ecstatic, excited, and enamored by the fact that God wanted to use me.

No one had shared the good news with me before. So I thought Yeshua-Jesus was some sort of avatar, God-man, or prophet. I thought He was one of many of the divine manifestations of God in human form that comes to show us the way.

Right after that, my best friend, John, started witnessing to me. He began to tell me, "Jesus is the Messiah, and if you don't believe in Him, you're going to go to hell." And I'm like, "Man, there are many ways to get into New York City—you can take the GW, the Lincoln Tunnel—there's lots of ways. It's just about being spiritual." Then John started to attend a Messianic congregation with Rabbi Jonathan Cahn. He called me and read me a passage from the Old Testament. I'd never heard that passage before in all the years I studied.

KATHIE LEE: Why not?

RABBI JASON: Jewish people read many passages from Isaiah, but not Isaiah 53. Some Jews don't read the entire Bible, and passages like Isaiah 53 were never taught.

KATHIE LEE: So you heard Isaiah 53, and what happened inside you?

RABBI JASON: I began to be provoked to jealousy. I had to know more about Jesus. I agreed to go with John to the Messianic service. At the end of the night, they dimmed the lights, and Rabbi Cahn began to lead a prayer for salvation. I figured I needed all the help I could get. I was looking for spiritual enlightenment, so I was more than happy to pray.

It was the first time I had ever prayed to Yeshua-Jesus, and the people said, "Those whose first time it was to pray to Yeshua, please raise your hands." I raised my hand. Then they announced, "If you raised your hand, please stand up—you've just been born again." I'm thinking, "*I gave my mom enough trouble being born once! I'm not getting born again.*" I'd heard about those born-again people. I'd seen them on TV, televangelists. Suddenly, a man from Brooklyn said to me, "If you can't stand for the Messiah here, then you won't be able to stand before the world." I realized we weren't going anywhere until I stood up. So I stood up, and after explaining to me about the decision I'd just made, they gave me the first New Testament I'd ever seen: *The New Covenant Prophecy Edition*, with the Messianic prophecies in it. My friend John was so happy that I came to know the Lord.

KATHIE LEE: Then what did you do?

RABBI JASON: After I got home, curiosity got the best of me, and I read the New Testament. In my house, pornography was better than the New Testament. I was blown away by the Jewishness of Jesus, the power of His words, and the fulfillment of all the promises from the Hebrew Scriptures. Then I discovered that what He had said to me in my encounter in heaven was actually a verse from the New Testament that I had never read in my entire life. When I read that in the Gospel of Matthew, I was like, "He's the one. He's the one our people have been waiting for!"

I hid the New Testament in my bedroom because God forbid my mom find it. And, of course, I should've learned you can't hide anything from your mom. She found the Bible in my bedroom. "Don't tell me you've become one of those Jews who believe in Jesus. I knew you'd do something like this one day and break my heart. You've joined a cult. You need to go meet with the rabbi."

In the midst of this, I received a call from a friend. I used to go into New York City and feed homeless people, so one guy I'd become friends with called me collect from NYU Medical Center. He had been sleeping outside in the winter, and he contracted frostbite. The hospital told him that his legs needed to be amputated. I went and saw him, and I had just read the book of Acts. I prayed for him and laid hands on him. He was healed, came to faith, and walked out of the hospital. So when I went to meet with the rabbi, I was like, "No one is going to convince me that Yeshua isn't the promised Messiah."

I opened my Tanakh, my Jewish Bible, and I underlined all the Messianic prophecies, and the rabbi and I had a long discussion. He asked me, "Why do you believe this?" I shared with him. He gave his answer as to why my interpretation was wrong, but one thing he could not answer was Daniel 9, about the seventy weeks of Daniel: from the issuing of a decree to restore and rebuild Jerusalem, until Messiah the Prince comes and is cut off, 483 years have been decreed. And I said to him, "Who else could've fulfilled this?" He did not have an answer other than he had to research it. He wrote me a letter saying, "Jews don't calculate dates in Daniel."

KATHIE LEE: Why wouldn't they calculate the dates in Daniel?

RABBI JASON: They don't want to calculate the dates because it would lead people astray. In other words, there were inconvenient truths.

KATHIE LEE: What was your mother's reaction after that?

RABBI JASON: My mom was very concerned. She would've rather I went to India to study with gurus than to believe in Jesus. But the great thing was that when I encountered Him, it was like water to wine. Overnight God began transforming me. My parents realized that my faith in Jesus didn't make me less Jewish; it made me more Jewish. I understood that all the traditions and holidays I had enjoyed as a kid were culturally meaningful, but now they took on a new life and meaning. As my parents saw the change on every level of my life, and my being more engaged and wanting to do more Jewish studies and wanting to do Shabbat and the holidays, they became supportive of me. Many years later, my mom said, "I always dreamed you'd become a rabbi, but I never told you because I didn't want to pressure you. I just didn't know you'd become this kind of rabbi."

KATHIE LEE: Where are your parents now in their faith journey? Have they come to know Yeshua?

RABBI JASON: I'd say my dad knows Yeshua, and my mom is in process. They listen to and attend everything I do. My mom has had some heart palpitations, and she was concerned. I said, "Mom, I love you, and I want to see you in heaven. You've got to receive Yeshua because that's the only way for sure you can know." She said, "Well, how do you know I haven't? I pray to Him every day."

KATHIE LEE: Why do you think your dad has received him?

RABBI JASON: Well, my dad and I are very close. He reads and studies all the books. He was reading my book *Mysteries of the Messiah*, asking me questions and trying to understand it. From my discussions with him, it's kind of what I see in his life.

KATHIE LEE: When I first met you, you were doing this work in the Muslim world. Tell a little bit about the work.

RABBI JASON: I moved to California because some of our friends started this educational institute. I thought this was my dream job. I went to a healing conference, and this person prayed for me. He said, "You wear many mantles, like Joseph." And God began to speak to me.

In Judaism, there's this idea of two messiahs, son of David and son of Joseph. Son of Joseph is the suffering lamb, and son of David is the lion. God said to me, "*You've known Me in the fellowship of My sufferings and not the power of My resurrection. You've known Me from rejection and going through difficult stuff, and you've loved Me through all that, but you haven't known Me and what it means to live in the fullness of victory and to help other people overcome.*"

God began to do a new work in my life. He said to me, "*I'm going to take you through a season of Joseph. I'm going to take you to the pits and the prisons. You're going to go through some loss, but when I purify and humble you, you will learn to truly depend on Me. Then I'll lead you into what I have truly called you to do.*" I began to go through the season of Joseph. I lost my job, and I went through this really tough season.

KATHIE LEE: And your wife left you.

RABBI JASON: Unfortunately, that was the second season of loss. Again, I'm grateful to God for what He did. God had to deconstruct me so that He could build me back in a way that was healthy so I could truly become a new creation. It was out of that experience that God ultimately gave the foundation for what we're doing.

Thinking back to your question about Muslims, I had the opportunity to speak in Detroit. There were fifty thousand people at Ford Field. The person who was managing the event called me and said, "Jason, how do you break the spirit of anti-Semitism?" I said, "It's the story of Ruth and Boaz, Jew and Gentile coming together." He asked me to come and share this story.

I went to Detroit and shared the story of Ruth and Boaz and how Jews and Gentiles can join forces and become an unstoppable worldwide force for transformation. Unexpectedly, a man in the audience took the mic and said, "I grew up Muslim. I grew up hating Jews. I came to this country as a terrorist. Jesus encountered me. He opened my eyes, changed my life, changed my perspective on the Jewish people." He bent down on one knee and said, "I repent and on behalf of the Arab people ask your forgiveness for our hatred toward the Jewish people." Then I bent down on one knee, and there was a moment of reconciliation and the power of God in the presence of God. People were weeping. It was an amazing, holy moment. It demonstrated the power of Isaac and Ishmael, the coming together of Jew and Gentile.

That experience birthed in me the understanding that the good news is good news for us on a personal level, but also, truly, the good news has the power to overcome the greatest conflicts in our world. Most public conflicts in our world are the Israeli-Arab conflicts. The only way to overcome that animosity is the gospel, Yeshua. Because of both Isaac and Ishmael, Jew and Arab, it's in Him that we can truly love one another, be family, and have genuine restoration. This reconciliation would be a powerful demonstration of the gospel.

So God gave me this heart for Arab believers. Arabs have so many misconceptions about Jews. We want to change the misconceptions. We want to show how Arabs and Jews, Muslims and Jews can love one another.

KATHIE LEE: So that's where the whole concept for your ministry, Fusion Global, came from, right? The old and new? That's just so profound.

RABBI JASON: Yes. Connection is an important part of Fusion. We want not only the connection of Jew and Gentile but for people to restore the lost connection to our ancient roots and rediscover their forgotten inheritance.

KATHIE LEE: Amazing. So God continued to reveal this whole ministry that came from the fact that you were chosen to do this work. And then I called you. What happened then?

RABBI JASON: Yeah. I remember where I was on the day you called me. I was at my son's baseball game. You said you were working on this project in Israel. I was coming to New York right around Christmas.

KATHIE LEE: I had to write a book, so I called you and asked for your help.

RABBI JASON: I loved that you saw when you study the Bible from a rabbinic perspective, it makes it come alive. So I was excited because that was my passion, and it was life-changing for me. Going to Israel was such a great trip, so much fun.

KATHIE LEE: My biggest takeaway was the fact that I was so wrong about people. I thought people didn't have any spiritual curiosity. They just seemed happy to live with their Christmas tinsel. It's the exact opposite of that. People are dying for truth.

RABBI JASON: I think the reality is that people have been given junk food. And when they taste a true meal of good food, the meat of the Word, it satisfies on such a deep level. That's why we've been teaching and discipling people and growing our ministry. At Fusion Global, we want to add definition to people's faith.

Also, we hope to help people discover how important Jesus felt the festivals, traditions, and Old Testament teachings were. We want people to grow spiritually and understand how important the festivals should be to us as followers of Yeshua.

We also want to expand people's understanding of prayer and Scripture to include ancient Hebrew and contemporary wisdom informed by the Spirit. When they do, they can enrich their perspective of Yeshua-Jesus and His teachings. They understand that their lives can overflow to abundance as they study, worship, pray, and know Yeshua.

SIXTEEN

A SPIRITUAL FAMILY CONNECTION

DAVID, KELLY, AND NICHOLAS POMERANZ

The year 2000 was a big one for me. I made my debut on Broadway in Stephen Sondheim's musical *Putting It Together.* I hosted *Late Night with David Letterman*, made a film with Howie Mandel called *Spinning Out of Control*, and released two albums: the pop album *Heart of a Woman* for Universal Records and *Born for You*—my favorite of all of the twenty-two I've recorded. Oh yes, I almost forgot! I also left *Live with Regis and Kathie Lee* after fifteen incredible years.

It was obviously a milestone year for me and one I look back on with extraordinary gratitude. I made amazing new friends, and one of them, the crazy-talented singer-composer David Pomeranz, is an even dearer friend today. David composed the title song "Born for You" with another equally talented friend and Tony-winning lyricist, David Zippel.

I invited David Pomeranz to visit me, and we wrote a song together. That was twenty-one years ago, and I have lost count of how many we have written since. Both my off-Broadway musical, *Under the Bridge*, and my

Tony-nominated *Scandalous* were written with David, as is one of my newest oratorios, *The God of the How and When*. I believe that gives you a good idea of how much I love and admire him.

David grew up in a Jewish family but is now a member of the Church of Scientology, which I had heard of but knew very little about. As the years and projects flew by, we shared many conversations about our spiritual beliefs, and I felt led to invite David and his wife, Kelly, and son, Nicholas, to accompany me on one of our rabbinical trips to Israel. As it always does, that trip changed everyone's hearts.

KATHIE LEE: So, Dave, you grew up with your beautiful parents in a Jewish home. Can you tell me about that?

DAVID: Well, I was very blessed because of these good, good people. It was a real family, a big tribe. The best part of my upbringing was the family coming together and enjoying one another. Spiritually, as you know, my dad and I would perform in the synagogue, and it was one of the first times I played in front of an audience.

KATHIE LEE: And that was in New York, right?

DAVID: Yes, it was in New York, in Long Island. And I was maybe nine or ten years old. We were in the choir, and on the High Holy Days, we would go to the mic and sing the most gorgeous—

KATHIE LEE: Yes. They are gloriously beautiful, they are ancient and from age to age, or everlasting. They are magnificent.

DAVID: That's the truth. So the music was something we all shared. We gathered around the Passover table with family, and we sang. We celebrated Hanukkah, and we sang. I was bar mitzvahed, and we sang. It wasn't so much about the literal Bible as it was a spiritual feeling that connected us all through the music.

KATHIE LEE: And then, David, you pursued a very successful career in music, working with artists like Barry Manilow. You and I met when I was doing my album *Born for You*. And then you met Kelly, and that's when your life changed. Am I right about that?

DAVID: Yes, you are right about that.

KATHIE LEE: Kelly, let's get to you for a second. You discovered something called Scientology. At what age were you?

KELLY: I was about twenty-four.

KATHIE LEE: What was it about Scientology that appealed to you?

KELLY: Well, I always knew I was a spiritual being. It was just taken for granted that there was another dimension in life. And I was raised Catholic and went to Catholic school. But after I got out of college, there were certain things in my life, certain barriers I was hitting up against, and I thought, "*There must be something that I don't know.*" And Scientology actually makes me a better Christian. All the goals that I had as a young person in my religion, I still have the same ones. I mean, Jesus, you know, He is the role model. He is the guy.

KATHIE LEE: Right.

KELLY: I just found Scientology had tools that made sense. Scientology doesn't tell you, "Here is something, and you have to believe this." It's like, "Here is a piece of information. When you apply this in life, see if it helps improve conditions." So it helps you toward your own goals.

A friend of mine told me about this place called Celebrity Centre, which helps artists, because Mr. Hubbard felt that artists create the society. I think artists have the ability and the courage to create new places and new viewpoints for people to move into.

KATHIE LEE: Yes, if we are created in God's image, then we are creators as well. And I think that's why as artists we feel such an overflowing in our spirits when we create something of beauty to share with a hurting world. It's got to be done for that purpose, too, right?

KELLY: Yeah, absolutely, because we are multifaceted beings. It's a joyful thing to be as godlike as we can, to use our talents as much as we can to improve life and to help others, and to be involved with others, which Jesus was.

KATHIE LEE: The Bible says "to whom much is given, much is required." We are to understand who God is, what He wants from His followers, not to control them but to bless them to bless others.

KELLY: And you have to allow others to have the blessing of giving also.

KATHIE LEE: So did you introduce David to Scientology, or did you find that on your own, David?

DAVID: No, I found it on my own. I was in a lot of spiritual pain and confusion and upset. And the beauty of Scientology for me is that it helped to handle the travail. I had my head screwed on straight enough to go, *Oh, I'm a spiritual being,* and then could live a more spiritual life and, as Kelly was saying, more and more, and closer and closer to God, and closer and closer to the all of all. And that's what it did for me.

KATHIE LEE: So this started working for you, and then you met Kelly there?

DAVID: Yeah, we met at a party and became good friends as artists, Kelly being a marvelous actress. We were interested in one another's art and our processes, and then we fell in love.

KATHIE LEE: And when I met you, David, you had adopted a baby boy, Nicholas. Tell me about that.

KELLY: Yeah, so the thing with Nicky was very interesting. David and I got married later than a lot of people. And we were running around the world and doing shows, and we created this company, and I was producing things. All of a sudden, it was kind of like, "Wait a minute," looking at the clock, "when are we going to have kids?"

KATHIE LEE: Right, like, "Oh yeah, we forgot something."

KELLY: Yeah, I had this moment where I thought, "*If I take nine months, is it really going to be something I'm going to miss?*" And I went, "*No. So let's just adopt.*" Now, I didn't know at the time that it usually takes a couple of years—

KATHIE LEE: It's a long gestation.

KELLY: No, I had no idea. So I was visiting a friend who lived in Las Vegas, and we sat down to have coffee and catch up. She said, "Kelly, what are you doing?" I said, "Well, David and I decided we should adopt a kid." She said, "Oh my God, you are the parents!" And I said, "What are you talking about?" She said, "I know this fourteen-year-old girl; she is eight months pregnant. And she hasn't been able to find parents. And here you are!"

So I went home and told David about it. We found this lawyer, and he said, "Listen, you better jump on this. I've been in this business for almost twenty-five years, and I've never heard a story like this. There is some hand guiding this." So we decided to go meet the girl. Then I get a call from my friend, and she said, "The mother found a family in Los Angeles, and they are coming down on Saturday."

KATHIE LEE: So now it's going to be almost an auction.

KELLY: Yes. David said, "Kelly, we are flying to Las Vegas on Friday night," because the other family was supposed to come down Saturday. So we went to Vegas, and I took this big press book of David's with the pictures and everything.

KATHIE LEE: Of course. Like, "You, too, could be introduced to Barry Manilow."

KELLY: Yes, exactly. So we met the girl, and she was absolutely adorable. We went to a restaurant, where people just stand up and sing. David was asked to sing, so he sang, came back, sat down. She was sitting directly opposite us, and she said, "I'm not going to LA tomorrow because you are the parents," and we both started crying. She said, "I know I'm just the instrument for you, but you are actually the parents." It was like a spiritual thing where she knew that we were meant to have this child.

KATHIE LEE: Right, what wisdom for a fourteen-year-old.

DAVID: And she came and lived with us for some time, because we knew it was going to happen soon.

KELLY: I had forgotten that part, yeah. She stayed with us, and he was supposed to be born in about three weeks. Then, all of a sudden, one morning she was up very early, and I thought, "*Well, that's different.*" We were making breakfast, and she went into labor. We took her to the birthing center, and she wanted her mom to be there. So we called her mom; her mom jumped on a plane in Vegas. And just as her mom got there, he was born.

KATHIE LEE: How many miracles, how much evidence do you need of God's love?

KELLY: Yeah. It was; it really was a miracle.

KATHIE LEE: And he is how old now?

DAVID: He is going to be twenty in a few months.

KATHIE LEE: Wow, all right, so that's the miracle. Now David and I started working together, and I invited you guys to come to Israel with me. I prayed that the Lord would lead me to invite people who wouldn't automatically be the people I would put together. And so the Lord placed around my heart that the three of you should come as a family. And you did. And tell me what you expected and what surprised you the most, Kelly, please.

KELLY: Well, I love traveling, and I love learning. But I really didn't expect the spiritual experience. And I think my whole earlier education, you know in Catholic school, with Bible stories and all of that, the Bible came alive for me. Sort of like I understood it in a different way, and it was very profound, the connection with the Bible and Jesus and what His lessons really were.

KATHIE LEE: Yes. And when Nicky jumped in the Jordan to be baptized, it was just thrilling. But that's the way we ended our ten-day trip. And we all came home, I think, transformed and changed in different kinds of ways. And that's what I love about a personal God. Every one of us who went there left with the deeper understanding of who we are as individuals and where we fit as a community into this world that God has created. And was that your experience, Dave?

DAVID: Yes. I took away many, many things, like the both of you just discussed. Just the undeniable resonance of the truth that went on there. But being raised a Jew, I was missing the connection. I didn't understand. What's the point of having Jesus when you've got God?

KATHIE LEE: Yes, yes.

DAVID: And what I saw for myself was the message that you are made in the image of God. So this is how I got it. God takes this earthly form and transmits into this earthly form and gives Him a message and says, "Show them how it's done."

KATHIE LEE: Oh, David, that's beautiful.

DAVID: And the other thing I walked away really stunned with, how much it impressed me, was who this being was. Jesus. And you know, the bravery, the unconditional love, and unconditional compliance with His own message that He received. Jesus' message is, "Yes, here I am, here is God," but it's also, "There you are, and you are like Me. You treat others the way you want to be treated. It's God in you. So you get to walk like Me, to whatever degree you misstep or cheat or look away, you'll have some travail, because that's just the way it goes. It's not like I'm going to do anything bad to you, but you'll do something bad to you."

KATHIE LEE: That is amazing. That is so true. God just wants to bless His children. The Ten Commandments are to bless His children and bring us home to where He always intended us to be, in the Father's house. Wow, you guys, I'm so grateful for you sharing what you shared today.

KATHIE LEE: Nicholas, you were adopted. That kind of love is so special. Love is a choice, and your parents made a choice to find you. And when that opportunity arose, they just got in a car to Vegas.

NICHOLAS: Yes, that's where my biological mother lives. Her mom was really good friends with my parents. That's how my parents ended up hearing about it.

KATHIE LEE: Your mom grew up Catholic, and your dad is Jewish. And they both had become members of Scientology by the time you were born. Tell me how that affected your young life.

NICHOLAS: From an early age, Scientology got me to be responsible for myself and my actions. The truth about Scientology is that it's a technology to life, covering areas like how to understand human emotions, why people do what they do, how to communicate more effectively, and how to improve relationships. I consider myself a Christian as well.

KATHIE LEE: Okay, so tell me, what was your first impression of Jesus?

NICHOLAS: Well, the first time I ever heard about Jesus was in third or fourth grade. I did a world religions class. All that I can recall then was how Jesus Christ lived over in the Middle East somewhere, and He'd cure people with leprosy, and go to women with scarlet letters and flow them love when no one else did. I didn't so much get into the religious side, but it was more about the miracles He did that intrigued me.

KATHIE LEE: So when you were invited to come on the trip to Israel, what did you think?

NICHOLAS: I was thrilled. Israel is the center of all religion, maybe the most important place on planet Earth. When you read anything on Christianity or Judaism, it's all about Israel.

KATHIE LEE: Yes, and even Islam. All roads lead to Israel. So what was your first impression of the land? Did you have a favorite spot?

NICHOLAS: Yes. Bethlehem.

KATHIE LEE: Tell me why.

NICHOLAS: I'm sure you experience a similar thing, a certain energy. Considering the most iconic figure in the history of modern humanity, Jesus Christ, was born there, where a lot of these miracles occurred, it was amazing being in the exact same presence where He was born.

KATHIE LEE: Where divinity became humanity. You were the youngest member of our team. I loved your openness. I didn't know how your family would respond. I knew your dad, David, as a Jew would respond magnificently to the Jewish stuff we were learning. We all came from the same earthly father, Abraham, but that the story from the Old Testament continues with the New Testament. It's one love story about how God created us for fellowship with Him. So to see you jump in the Jordan, there was an eagerness about you, and you were the first one. What were you thinking on that day?

NICHOLAS: It's one thing to get baptized in Florida or New York or Chicago, but baptized in the Jordan River? I just thought it was an amazing opportunity. And my dad being Jewish, my mom being Christian, and us being Scientologists has nothing to do with being in the Holy Land.

I was superexcited to get baptized and immerse myself in everything that was going on.

KATHIE LEE: Has it changed you at all?

NICHOLAS: I would say that the trip in general changed me. Learning about Jesus' tenure for thirty-three years gave me a lot more of reality about Christianity. It's hard to know what's true and false about religions in particular, especially with the media being extremely biased. Going to Israel, and hearing pretty much from the source, gave me a profound reality of Christianity and how these events transpired. It gave me an exterior view of the world.

KATHIE LEE: It certainly broadens it. So for your young heart, Jesus met you right where you were so you could understand Him because He longs to have you walk with Him and be your Messiah, best friend, and your source of life. As you go forward, I have no doubt in my heart, what God did in you during that time He will continue to work in you.

SEVENTEEN

RESCUED BY LOVE

JIMMY WAYNE

When I first heard country artist Jimmy Wayne's story from my friend Anne Neilson, I couldn't believe anyone could emerge triumphant from such an abusive, tragic, and hopeless childhood. Then I met Jimmy, and he told me much more than Anne had shared.

It was hard to associate this handsome, charming, sweet man with an easy laugh with the one I had heard about. The difference, as usual, was the power of his personal faith in his heavenly Father.

KATHIE LEE: What was your earliest recollection of hearing Jesus' name or picturing Him?

JIMMY: My first memory of Jesus was when I was five years old. I received a collection of Bible books, and I loved looking at the illustrations. The second time was when I hung myself on the cross. I went to vacation Bible school, and up until this point I'd been taught the fear: "If you do wrong, you'll be punished." I associated Jesus with that, but the vacation Bible school teacher taught about the love of Jesus. I was so into it. That's the first time I really learned and put it together that Jesus is representative of pure love. And then I was so compassionate about that story she told that I decided I wanted to know how He felt. So I built a cross in the yard and hung myself on it. And that's when it started. That seed was planted right there.

KATHIE LEE: Guess where my daddy came to know Jesus as a little Jewish boy at eight years old? Vacation Bible school.

JIMMY: Wow. I didn't want to go because I thought they beat kids up. I was afraid to go. I think people are afraid to talk about Jesus because they associate the name *Jesus* with people who do those sorts of things.

KATHIE LEE: Very good point. Your life became unraveled because of your mom's lifestyle and mental illness. You saw that she did love Jesus in her own way, didn't she?

JIMMY: Mom was really conflicted, but she loved Jesus. She learned about Jesus from her mom. Her mom was very grounded in Jesus. My mom was bipolar. She would go all-in—church, dress, no makeup. But then she'd be wearing tight jeans, drinking, cussin' in the street. As soon as she would make one little mistake, she'd throw her hands up and go drink a whole bottle of liquor. Her fear of letting Him down. I'd say, "Mom, He forgives you for that."

KATHIE LEE: You sound like you were the parent. Even though you were having your own issues, you knew that Jesus would forgive her? Where did that come from?

JIMMY: I don't know. We went to church when we were living with this stepdad or that boyfriend; we were drug around from church to church. I knew He existed. My mom had not just planted that seed in my head, but she practically beat that seed in my head that "This is real, and don't ever doubt it. You're going to believe this, one way or another."

KATHIE LEE: So in her own weird way, she was doing that out of love for you?

JIMMY: To her, it was like, "I'm doing something good for you." It was weird. "I'm hitting you because I love you."

KATHIE LEE: So she didn't have any concept of grace?

JIMMY: No, not until she got medicated. She was a completely different human being.

KATHIE LEE: Well, let's continue on the faith journey. You lived on the streets. Where was Jesus when you were thirteen years old and left at the bus station?

JIMMY: Believe it or not, I was talking to Him, and I was cussing and yelling at Him. I was like, "I can't believe You keep allowing this to happen." I was blaming Him for everything. I became really angry with Jesus. It didn't make sense to me. I remember lying in my bed—an army cot I had pulled out of a junk pile and put plastic on it—and it was so cold. I knew that Jesus could hear me, I believed, and I was mad. I was like, "I'm in a cold, abandoned trailer. I've not done anything wrong to deserve this."

KATHIE LEE: How long were you homeless?

JIMMY: The first time, when I was fourteen, it was a couple of months. The second time, when I was sixteen, it was a couple of months.

KATHIE LEE: You never stopped believing, even through all of that? Did you?

JIMMY: I almost looked at Him like He was my mom. She loved me, but then she'd hit me. And so I was like, "*That must be what parents do. She must be doing what He does.*" So I was like, "*I know You love me, but You're really mean to me.*"

KATHIE LEE: So what age were you when you met Bea and Russell, the couple who would change your life? Where were you on your faith walk?

JIMMY: I was sixteen, in North Carolina. I was living outside and couch surfing. I was not a big guy, but I was having to fight different people in the neighborhood. That was taking a physical toll because I wasn't doing anything wrong, but these people were just picking. And on top of that, I was having to find food. I still knew He was there, but it was an "I wish You loved me back the way I love You."

KATHIE LEE: Wow. Did you feel like a wounded animal at times?

JIMMY: I think that's the mentality; you're so broken down, and you don't make the right choices, and the only thing you're thinking about is "*I* *need to find food, and I don't want to get in trouble with anybody, and I just want to stay out of the way.*"

I knew my future was spiraling down. I felt in my heart, "*I'm not going to be anything other than this.*" It was really depressing. *Hopelessness* is the perfect word because I didn't know how to get out. So when I met Bea and Russell, the voice that spoke to me all the time when I was a kid, it spoke to me that day to turn around.

I was riding a bike past the woodshop. I looked over and saw a man cutting wood on a band saw. And that voice told me, "*Go in and ask if he has any work you could do.*" I turned the bike around and leaned it up against the woodshop. I went up and said, "Sir, do you have any work I could do?" The old man said, "Ask the boss," nodding toward this white-haired lady. She turned off the saw, put her goggles on top of her hair, brushed her arms off. She walked toward me, brushing off her apron. She said, "Do you cut grass?" I said, "Yes, ma'am, but I don't have a lawn mower." She said, "We have one." She looked at her watch and said, "Come back and cut our grass at five o'clock." So I came back at four thirty and was just sitting outside, waiting on her to get off of work. I didn't want to be late.

She came out of the house while I was cutting the grass, and then she walked over to this fence and motioned for me to come over to the fence. She paid me twenty dollars, and she gave me a Coca-Cola. I remember thinking that was a lot of money. She let me use her lawn mower, her fuel, and she gave me twenty dollars. It was amazing! Then she said come back next week. So now I had a permanent job cutting her grass, the Coca-Cola, and twenty dollars.

Toward the end of the summer, the grass wasn't growing as much because it was getting cool. I was cutting, and she motioned for me to come to the fence. I pulled over, and she gave me a Coca-Cola and a donut stick. She had a very concerned look and asked, "Jimmy, where do you live?" I didn't want to tell her. I was sixteen, my hair was down past my collarbone, and I was wearing the same clothes every week. I told her, "I live up the road from here." I felt like if I told her I was homeless, she wouldn't want me around her house. She said, "Well, Russell and I have been talking, and we want to know if you'd be interested in moving into our home."

So I left that day, went and got my stashed clothes, and came back that evening. The first thing I remember stepping into her home was how it smelled. It smelled like she was baking something in the oven, like a pie. It smelled like home.

I walked across the living room, and I didn't make eye contact with Russell. I didn't like men, and I sure didn't like for them to tell me what to do. Russell didn't do anything to me, but my experience with men up to that point was that's what you do.

About three or four days into it, I was coming out of the bedroom. I remember Russell putting his hand on my shoulder and saying, "I need to talk to you about something." I knew he was going to make me leave. He said, "Sit down." He held up three fingers and said, "Jimmy, if you're going to stay in my home, there's two things you've got to do." I wanted to tell him he was holding up three fingers, but that voice told me this was when I should probably keep my mouth closed. "The first thing you've got to do is cut off all your hair, and it has to be just like mine." And then he lowered one finger. "We want you to go to church." And he lowered the second finger. "And if you don't do those two things, you've got to leave now." Russell lowered the third finger. I stayed there six years. That's winning the lottery! They gave me minimum resources, a place to live, and an opportunity to work. I mean, it changed my life.

Three months after I moved in, Russell died. He had cancer. No one knew it. Bea walked out of the house and saw me standing in the yard. She said, "I want you to stay here if you want to stay. I believe you were sent here." In my mind, I'm like, "*Wow.*" She said, "You don't have to if you don't want to." I said, "No, I'll stay. I don't have anywhere else to go."

KATHIE LEE: She got it all from the Bible, all from God.

JIMMY: She was so grounded in the Word. I mean, she read every single day. She carried her Bible; she'd read it at any event. She didn't play politics, and she didn't push it on you. She just would read and then go on about her business.

KATHIE LEE: Then Bea died. That's when everything changed. Tell me about after Bea died.

JIMMY: There's no way that a human could time it this way. When Bea passed, that very month, I received a phone call from the Opryland Music Group and was invited to move to Nashville and start writing songs. It was like, "Wow, man, everything I loved was here, but now Bea died." During the time up until she died, I was doing karaoke, singing at cookouts and weddings. She'd always go with me to these events. Everywhere I'd go, there was this white-haired lady with me. She'd show up with me, sit down, read Scripture. I'd do my gig. Afterward, I'd say, "Bea, you ready to go?" and she'd say, "Okay."

KATHIE LEE: You started taking care of her.

JIMMY: Yeah, and at one of those events, she was sitting in the front row reading her Scripture. I told her, "You may want to sit over here so we can get out easier." My plan was to get her out of the fan zone because there were a lot of pretty girls there. I went backstage, and the announcer introduced me, and I ran onstage—and Bea had put herself back over in the section with the fans.

KATHIE LEE: She put a damper on the evening, didn't she? Ha ha.

JIMMY: She'd read, and I'd sing. On the way home that day, I heard that familiar voice speak to me again, and it said, "*Tell her you love her.*" But I thought, "*Man, I'm so uncomfortable saying that.*" I was about a minute away from dropping her off, and I said, "Bea, I love you." She turned to look at me and said, "I love you, too, Jimmy." That was the first time I ever said those words to her. I think it shocked her. I said, "Bea, I know I wouldn't be here had it not been for you. I wouldn't be driving this car, I wouldn't have these clothes, I wouldn't have an education, this job." I remember thanking her for everything I could possibly think of.

I pulled in her driveway, jumped out of the car, and helped her out of the car. She was eighty-one years old. As soon as she got out of the car, she grabbed her right leg. I said, "Are you okay?" She said, "I just got this pain in my leg." I remember walking her real slow, and she was kind of limping to the glass storm door. I said, "Bea, I'll be back in three days." She said, "Goodbye, Jimmy." I said, "Goodbye, Bea." She said, "Goodbye, Jimmy." She kept saying it. I kept saying it too. I started walking backward, waving. She was yelling it and smiling and laughing at the same time. Like some kind of going-away celebration. I got in the car and threw my hand out the window while I was waving. I could hear, "Goodbye, Jimmy!" And that was it. The next morning her daughter called me and said she had a stroke. The blood clot was in her leg and moved to her brain.

KATHIE LEE: She knew.

JIMMY: I mean, I think she knew. I really believe God gave me that opportunity to tell her I loved her.

KATHIE LEE: Oh, Jimmy. This woman, she mirrored Christ's love to you. Tell me about what you found out at the funeral.

JIMMY: I thought I was this random kid they wanted to help out. But at her funeral, I saw all these strange faces in the pews. I went up to Bea's daughter after the funeral and asked her who these people were. She was like, "Oh, that's so-and-so. Mom and Dad took her in when she was a teenage girl, and that's her and her family now. Oh, that's such-and-such. Mom and Dad took him in back in the eighties, and that's him and his family now." So these stories started coming out. Russell and Bea had spent their entire adult lives taking people in and helping get them on their feet. I was just one of them.

KATHIE LEE: The impact of one beautiful angel of God seeing the purpose in a raggedy little boy, and she gave you a home. It's the greatest gift anyone can ever give. I love you for sharing this story.

JIMMY: I love sharing her story. I've seen how it has affected people all over the country. Bea was so incredible.

KATHIE LEE: She's a hero of faith. Every one of us is humbled by her. That's a Christian. Lord, give us eyes to see the need around us and take the time to try and help them.

EIGHTEEN

OUR COMMON GROUND IS SACRED GROUND

RAAKHEE MIRCHANDANI

I met Raakhee Mirchandani in New York City in 2012, when she breathlessly dropped into her seat at my table at Neary's pub, where I was already seated with the editor of the *New York Daily News*, Colin Myler, Raakhee's boss.

She was newly pregnant at the time, and I instantly warmed to this inquisitive and lively, obviously brilliant young woman. Hoda and I eventually began to write a weekly column for the paper, and we began a beautiful friendship that continues today. I wanted to include Raakhee's story because it is so different and interesting, just like she is.

KATHIE LEE: We met around nine years ago. Tell me about your background spiritually.

RAAKHEE: I was born in New Jersey to Indian immigrants. My parents emigrated from India to the United States. My grandparents were refugees because of the India-Pakistan partition in 1947, so spirituality was baked into everything we did, every conversation we had with our parents and grandparents. We knew in our hearts that what carried my grandparents safely from country to country, and my parents safely from country to country, was God, and that God made a space for them in this world. It was on all of those prayers, from my ancestors and my grandparents, that my life and my family's life came to be so blessed.

KATHIE LEE: And you grew up in a Hindu home, right?

RAAKHEE: Yes, my parents are Hindu, but because of the community that we're from, it's called Sindhi. It's Hindu with very strong Sikh influences.

KATHIE LEE: Thus, your husband's influence as well?

RAAKHEE: Yes, Sikh. Yes.

KATHIE LEE: So in the Hindu religion, there are many gods. It's polytheistic, right?

RAAKHEE: Yes. That's right.

KATHIE LEE: Tell me what that meant to you.

RAAKHEE: So this is the way my parents would explain it to me, and I still very much believe this: God is God. There's one God, and there's all these different forms that appeal to different people. So if the goddess is appealing to you, if Ganesha the elephant god is appealing to you, if Krishna is appealing to you, then that's what you worshiped and invited into your heart and your home. The essence of God, or the idea of God, was one, but the forms were many, as the paths are many to sort of attain that salvation that we were seeking.

KATHIE LEE: Okay, so this was powerful in your life, this whole concept?

RAAKHEE: It was extremely powerful in my life. I didn't really spend time to understand the difference between religion and spirituality, and quite frankly, I'm not sure I still understand the difference because they're really intertwined in my life. I also went to Catholic school for a couple of years as a kid. It was very formative for me because I felt like it didn't feel separate from the faith my parents were teaching me at home. It felt like a reaffirming and a confirmation of what I knew in my heart, which was that God is real, and God is in my life every single day.

KATHIE LEE: It's so interesting that you find the two compatible.

RAAKHEE: It always worked for me. For me, I'm the kind of person when it comes to these sorts of things, I look for confirmation. I meet people, and I find goodness in them. We may disagree on ten things and we may agree on two, but in those two I think there can be real power. So, for me, that's the connection point and that's the shared humanity. And I believe that's what God is in people.

KATHIE LEE: It's like our common ground is our sacred ground.

RAAKHEE: Totally.

KATHIE LEE: So you and I and Hoda met at Neary's pub. And we began a friendship, and we became colleagues when Hoda and I started to have our funny little column.

RAAKHEE: That seems like a lifetime ago.

KATHIE LEE: When you and I first met, I started sharing with you about my rabbinical studies. What do you remember about that?

RAAKHEE: I remember when we first met after Neary's, I came to the greenroom. I must've been three or four months pregnant at the time. I was nervous, I was young, and I was at the *Today* show. I didn't know you then, and what I found so interesting in that moment, your care for me, someone who you just met, told me so deeply who you were and how you see people. And as we got to know each other, the thing I thought was most fascinating was the way you talked about Israel. I think you said your dad had taken you there as a kid for your first time?

KATHIE LEE: Yes, he sent my mom and me there as a high school graduation present.

RAAKHEE: That's right! Agan and I had been trying to go to Israel. It just didn't work out because of the politics of the passport. I was desperate to go. I thought it was so interesting that after so many years of trying to go, within just a couple of years of you and me being friends, we actually made that trip happen.

KATHIE LEE: Tell me, what were your first impressions when you got there?

RAAKHEE: I had come off a really tough time. My daughter had been sick with cancer for the first year of her life. So the trip came at a time when she was healthy and I was trying to piece back together parts of my life and parts of my relationship with Agan. It's really hard to be married when you think that your child, your newborn, is going to die. We clung together, and I clung to faith as I normally do. I remember when we got to Israel, there were two parts in particular that I thought, "*I need to be here because I need this in my life just now.*"

KATHIE LEE: What were they?

RAAKHEE: The first one was when we were walking at Ein Gedi, where the waterfall is. We were sitting there, and Rod had us read a part of the Bible. And I don't know how to read a Bible. He was saying names and numbers, and I was like, "Why aren't you giving us page numbers? How am I supposed to find things?" And then, of course, he kept calling on me to read, and I was like, "I don't know where you are, Rod! I don't understand where I am in the book!" He had me read something, and there are two pieces that I still remember. Something about living water.

KATHIE LEE: Yes, streams of living water.

RAAKHEE: I remember being really touched by that idea at that moment. And the other thing was that I sensed true, intense power when we were in Israel. We had gone on a little hike, I think in the Valley of Elah. I had never read the story. Of course, I'd heard of David and Goliath, like in the Malcolm Gladwell sense. In many ways that story was made just for me, at that moment in my life. I believe that if we really listen to what's happening around us, God speaks very clearly to us. And I felt like I was being spoken to very clearly.

KATHIE LEE: How much did it matter that you were in the place where that event occurred?

RAAKHEE: Agan and I talked about that a lot. Because I felt in Israel very similar to the way that I feel when I'm in India. For me, I think it's because really important things have happened there for centuries, and I think that lots of those energies and those whispered prayers hang in the air there, and I felt them really deeply. It meant everything to be there. I think if you'd said, "Hey, Raakhee, let's read David and Goliath while we're sitting in New York," I'd be like, "No." I mean, if you told me to do it, I probably would, but I don't think it would've worked in my heart the way that it did there.

KATHIE LEE: There's such a connection with the ancient there.

RAAKHEE: I think there's something to this idea, right? It's a place that people have been living and praying and doing for centuries, and I think that energy hangs everywhere. And it's for you, if you're open to it.

KATHIE LEE: And you really sense the presence of God there, and the ancients.

RAAKHEE: I agree.

KATHIE LEE: Tell me your first thought of Jesus. What were you first taught about Jesus as a child?

RAAKHEE: My parents are very religiously and spiritually free, so we were exposed to lots of different religions and beliefs. As a young girl, I had books about Buddha and books about Jesus. We watched *The Ten Commandments* every year. My parents went to Catholic school; it's a common practice in India. I started my schooling in Catholic school, so I was pretty familiar with Jesus. Like, I knew the Our Father at the same time I learned Hindu prayers. They were both on my tongue at the same time. It never felt separate for me. God always felt the same; it all felt like the same. It wasn't like, "This God is your God, and this one is mine." It all just felt like, "This one is my God."

KATHIE LEE: And you weren't at all threatened by Him?

RAAKHEE: Never, not at all.

KATHIE LEE: And did you learn anything about Him that changed your perception?

RAAKHEE: I was quite familiar with religion, but the thing that I learned in Israel, and was surprised by, was to have a window into other people's relationships with God. I think about how we stopped on the side of the road by the river Jordan, we had to walk up a little bit. People were going to be baptized—which I thought you just got baptized as a kid. I didn't know people did that as adults. I tried to find a place that was out of the way. Of course, in trying to move out of the way, I ended up having a front-row seat.

KATHIE LEE: You sure did. You ended up having to help people in!

RAAKHEE: Literally! I put all this stuff on myself that I want to be out of the way. Of course, that was not the plan God had for me. God's plan was, "You will witness all of this, you will help everybody in and out, you will have a front-row seat because there's something in this experience for you too." And I don't think things happen accidentally.

KATHIE LEE: Did you know in the Hebrew language, there's no word for *coincidence*? God is either sovereign God, or He is not God at all.

RAAKHEE: That is a very Indian, Hindu philosophy. Everything is for a reason. All of it. Maybe you don't understand it today, but that doesn't mean it doesn't have a reason. I've unpacked that experience a lot for myself because it was so interesting to me.

KATHIE LEE: I've spoken to quite a few of us who were on that trip. The first one in the Jordan River was a young man who grew up in Scientology, and the last one was someone I've been praying for, for thirty years, my stepdaughter, Vicki. Was there ever a moment when you thought that you might like something like that in your life, that cleansing?

RAAKHEE: No, because I felt like it was very much my experience but in a different way. It was the way it was supposed to be for me.

KATHIE LEE: Well, God is such a custom-made God.

RAAKHEE: Yes.

KATHIE LEE: And at the very end of it, at the last day, when we were all offered Communion at the Garden of Gethsemane, did you take Communion that day?

RAAKHEE: We didn't.

KATHIE LEE: Tell me why.

RAAKHEE: I felt like there were rules around what you had to do, certain things, in order to go through the Communion process, and I never did any of that, so I didn't want to disrespect anyone.

KATHIE LEE: That's interesting. That is part of the Catholic faith but not part of the Protestant faith. So that was totally a part of what you learned.

RAAKHEE: Totally. I don't want to disrespect anyone. I take that pretty seriously. Not just when it comes to God and religion. Just in general, I don't want to disrespect people. That's not my vibe, not how I want to live my life.

KATHIE LEE: That's interesting. For me, so much of what I share is about the difference between religion and relationship with a living God. Did any of that make any more sense or less sense during your trip?

RAAKHEE: I've heard you say this to me a lot during our friendship, so I had thought about that concept before. And my parents had spoken about it before too. As a believer, I don't subscribe to a lot of the rules as much as I subscribe to the way I want to live my life in service. The way I worship God is that I live my life in service to other people in my community and other people who need an extra hand. Faith looks like a lot of different things in everyone's lives. It gave me comfort in knowing people experience this differently. It's not like you have to do these ten things if you're a good person, a religious person.

KATHIE LEE: Not a one-size-fits-all.

RAAKHEE: Exactly. For me, that window, in watching other people, gave me that sense of what relationship looks like for others in action. And I loved that.

KATHIE LEE: When you talk about how you want to live your life in service, do you think you're really describing the essence of Jesus?

RAAKHEE: Service, right? Yeah, this is a very big concept in Sikhism; it's called *seva*. It's like a central tenet, and it means service. It's to be in service to yourself and to others, and that's how we honor and praise God.

KATHIE LEE: Do unto others as you would have them do unto you. Love your neighbor as you love yourself.

RAAKHEE: For me, I take that incredibly seriously, and I live that out every day. That's how I practice my faith.

KATHIE LEE: So what was your takeaway? Did the trip change anything or everything?

RAAKHEE: I think there were factors that led that to be the exact right time. A lot of things had to have happened for Agan and me to be there. Agan wasn't supposed to come, and then the thing he was supposed to do got canceled. For us to be there together, at that critical juncture in our marriage and our parenting journey, and going through some real trauma together, I think it changed a lot of things. We were connecting with each other; it made us talk about different things before we went to bed. I think it changed a lot of things for us.

I don't know that it changed me spiritually. I think it reconfirmed a lot of things that I believed, but I think that it deepened some understandings for me. And I think it also brought more faith into my life that I'm not sure what would've happened otherwise. I was deep into a life trauma. Hoda always says, "There's a handful of times that you're on your knees." I was really on my knees. I told Agan, "Who would've thought that a handful of folks looking for Jesus were going to be a part of my story?" But there it was.

KATHIE LEE: That's called God meeting our need right where it happens, where divinity and humanity intersect. Did you feel God's love while you were there from the people you were with, and also by being in that place?

RAAKHEE: I have very rarely not felt what I would describe as God's love. I have felt it in the happiest times of my life and in the darkest times of my life. Even when Satya was sick, I never felt forsaken or alone. I have always felt that.

I was telling Agan that the thing I felt there, the only way I can describe it, is the way that I feel in India, where there are some places we are just more deeply free of the world and more connected into ourselves and into God. And I felt that in Israel, in the exact same way that I felt in India. I find it really intoxicating, and it's why I really want to go back. I felt things there, and was compelled to talk about things there, that I don't necessarily get that same opportunity in myself here. There is something special that exists there, in a way like I feel in India where it's easier to look inside.

KATHIE LEE: It creates a very inviting environment. It invites you into a place of surrender of the spirit.

RAAKHEE: Totally, and I think that observing, on the Sabbath, our Jewish brothers and sisters having a really important moment at the Western Wall, and seeing our Muslim brothers and sisters praying also, I just think there was something really important. I don't have all the words for it, but I think you can feel it.

KATHIE LEE: Thus, the need for the next trip. The journey continues.

RAAKHEE: The journey continues.

NINETEEN

A JOURNEY OUT OF ATHEISM

ROGER CHARLES

On September 18, 2020, a group of Californians came to my home. My dear friend Angie Clawson had invited them because they were all contemplating a move from LA to Tennessee for various reasons. Roger Charles and his beautiful wife, Cynthia Garrett, were among them. Roger is one of the world's most accomplished architects, and he was designing a magnificent new development on thirty-eight hundred acres of Tennessee land.

As I welcomed them all with a glass of GIFFT wine and took them on a tour of my home, I was able to catch the excitement in them about starting a brand-new life in a brand-new place. I had done the exact same thing just three years before, and I wanted to be as helpful and kind to all of them as Angie and her husband, Greg, had been to me when I first arrived there.

Roger was a native Californian from Long Beach who grew up during the Jesus Movement, as I did. I love his story because he set out to disprove the existence of God, with surprising results.

KATHIE LEE: Roger, you have one of the most amazing testimonies in that you came out of a world of atheism.

ROGER: Yes, that's true.

KATHIE LEE: Where do you want to start with your story?

ROGER: Yes. There are so many factors that go into that whole story. Logically, I just believed there was no God from everything I saw. I'd been listening to all of the experts . . . or, at least, who I thought were experts. I lived in Long Beach in 1970, when the Jesus Movement happened in Orange County. It just exploded.

KATHIE LEE: How old were you at that time?

ROGER: I was ten or eleven. While I was in high school, my friends were becoming Christians, and my brother's friends were becoming Christians. I was getting asked a lot about God and Jesus. I didn't think any of them knew what they were talking about, but I didn't have any evidence to say they were wrong.

KATHIE LEE: You knew something was happening.

ROGER: It was very clear, but I was still young. To me, becoming a Christian sounded like believing the story your parents told you when they had to flush your pet goldfish. Christianity sounded like, "There is this great Daddy in the sky, and He created everything, but He has a problem now, and we're all going to die for it. But don't worry—He sent His Son to die for us and save us. But you can't talk to Him because He's gone to Daddy heaven so He can take care of all our no-nos. So everything is good now . . . if we just believe." It sounded like a fairy tale.

Anyway, all these people were talking about Jesus. I just didn't have the answers. I said, "Look, all the experts agree, Jesus never existed. Most of the Bible never happened." Finally, I decided, "Nobody has put together the definitive work on why the Bible is unreliable," so that's what I set out to do.

I realized I had no forum to prove things true or false. Without God, there is no purpose, and a universe without purpose is meaningless. So I had to find a philosophy to prove things true or false.

KATHIE LEE: You didn't even know where to start.

ROGER: It was crazy. So I started reading philosophers, and I got stuck on Descartes, the father of modern philosophy. He got rid of all the history of man's beliefs and everything we know and started proving our existence and purpose from there. Descartes was a Christian, but I liked him because he set aside his preconceived beliefs, including Christianity and the Bible.

Proving anything came down to only two things that are reliable: tangible evidence and reliable witnesses. It's like a court of law. If you can put tangible evidence on the table, great. If you can put a reliable witness on the stand, great. Those are the only two things you can prove anything by. With that, I was set to disprove the Bible.

KATHIE LEE: You were how old at this time?

ROGER: Seventeen. So I decided to take all the things that were on my evidence table against the Bible and start proving each of them. One of the things Descartes talked about was going to the source and not trusting what others said about evidence, which meant I had to read the Bible.

KATHIE LEE: Best thing you did.

ROGER: Definitely. Then I had to get context. So I read both sides. I read atheist authors, and I read Christian authors. And the Christian authors didn't sound quite as stupid as I thought they would.

KATHIE LEE: The usual suspects from that time: C. S. Lewis, Josh McDowell, Philip Yancey?

ROGER: Yes. I was reading all the evidence for and against. And at this point, I was trying to prove all of it is false because I was sure there was no God.

KATHIE LEE: You were still thinking you could do this?

ROGER: The Bible has over forty authors who wrote over two thousand years. I figured, "There's not five people over two thousand years who are going to agree on any subject, let alone God." I thought there would be contradictions everywhere. There were guys who appeared to be very good scholars, PhDs, and they wrote books on the contradictions in the Bible. The only problem is, I answered all of them at seventeen. There isn't a contradiction in the Bible.

KATHIE LEE: How could you know that without knowing the Greek and the Hebrew?

ROGER: Some of it is superobvious. I'll give you a classic example. In the Old Testament, it talks about the dimensions of the laver in the temple. It's a large bowl. In the Bible, when you read that in 1 Kings 7, the circumference is exactly three times larger than the diameter, but we all know pi is 3.14, et cetera. So the critics say, "The Bible is inaccurate." But further on, the Bible gives the thickness of the lip on the laver. When you adjust for the lip, the dimensions equal pi.

KATHIE LEE: Evidence.

ROGER: All of a sudden, the evidence against it becomes the evidence for it. That's what kept happening to me. I started off with archaeology. The first thing I had was the city of Tyre. Ezekiel made a prophecy about what was going to happen to the city of Tyre. And it turns out, archaeologists, when they finally discovered the city of Tyre, everything was exactly the way that Ezekiel talked about it. Ezekiel 26 says the city would be flat like the top of a rock, only good for fishermen to mend their nets on. And sure enough, there were fishermen mending their nets on what looked like a flat rock, but it's actually the pavement for the street.

KATHIE LEE: Right as he said it would be.

ROGER: So I freaked out and thought I would try a different way of proving the Bible wrong.

KATHIE LEE: Move on to the next thing . . .

ROGER: The next thing was to try to find Bible verses that contradicted. So I took all the experts and their Bible contradiction verses. Every time I dug into a supposed contradiction, I found out their criticism turned out to be evidence for the Bible. All my evidence against the Bible had whittled down to hardly anything, and the other evidence table had been stacked to the moon with evidence for the Bible.

So now I was sitting there thinking, "*I have way more evidence for the Bible than against the Bible.*" I had read the Bible three times at this point. And, of course, the Holy Spirit started working in me. The Bible was starting to make sense.

KATHIE LEE: Even things like the virgin birth and the resurrection of Jesus from the dead?

ROGER: Here's the problem. There are a lot of miracles in the Bible, and, of course, you can't prove them one way or another. Virgin birth being one of them. We just don't have the gynecology report from her doctor that says, "Yes, Mary, you're a virgin and pregnant." There are certain things you can't prove one way or another, but there are other things you can, and we do have witnesses. "Are they reliable enough?" becomes the issue. I wasn't concerned as to whether the Bible was Scripture or God-breathed. I was concerned as to whether it was reliable.

KATHIE LEE: At that time.

ROGER: Well, of course, because all that matters for Jesus to be true is that it's reliable. If I know I have great history on a situation from four, five, six, seven, eight witnesses, which is what the New Testament is, then can I trust those witnesses? And you've got somebody like Luke, who writes like any historian of his day, taking down other people's testimonies, like Stephen or Philip. All of a sudden, you have more witnesses. Like Apollo. You have all these witnesses, and to be an atheist, you have to prove they are all unreliable. The truth is, you can't prove any of them unreliable. Nobody has done that.

KATHIE LEE: When you know that the world changed hugely by their testimony.

ROGER: These guys spread a message to all the nations of the world because, at that time, the nations of the world were the Roman Empire, and a little bit beyond that. In their lifetime, within a hundred years, they had spread the gospel and become a religion in every nation, which is what Jesus told them to do. One of the things I learned as an atheist is the Bible is very specific.

KATHIE LEE: Nothing random about it.

ROGER: Every little detail becomes incredibly important, especially when you believe you have evidence and reliable witnesses. The more you pick apart details in the Bible, the more the Bible has the evidence and witnesses.

KATHIE LEE: It always has the answer.

ROGER: If you are determined to dig to the bottom, you'll get your answer, and that answer will blow away your doubts.

KATHIE LEE: At what age did you finally say, "Okay, I believe," and did you get down on your knees? Did you have some sort of a revelation? What happened?

ROGER: It was a full year later. I just was angry that I lost the battle and that the experts I trusted were liars. I threw away the Bible and went on to live my life like an idiot. Proving that God exists doesn't mean you know God.

KATHIE LEE: That's fascinating.

ROGER: About three months later, I was looking back at my life because most of my plans either failed or succeeded but with horrible results. I was thinking, *"I've proved that God exists, the Bible is true, and God loves me and has a plan for me. Also, He lives outside the time domain, which means He knows the future and has perfect plans. Why don't I want to know Him?"*

KATHIE LEE: Why wouldn't you want the better plan?

ROGER: I was an idiot. At this point, I hadn't been to a church. I just said, "God, I know You're real." I started praying every day, but my prayers felt like they were bouncing off the ceiling.

I understood there was a Holy Spirit, but I didn't know what that meant. In my mind, I thought it was like a shazam moment, because that's what it appears to be in the Bible, people have these shazam moments. So I started praying. I kept telling God that He could come along with me in my life. But nothing happened. After a few weeks, I finally said to God, "I know You won't reject me, so I will live my life for You, with or without a shazam moment." That's when it happened.

KATHIE LEE: That's precious.

ROGER: I walked out of my bedroom, and *boom*, peace just came in my life.

All of a sudden, I was sharing Jesus. I was like, "God is amazing," and people's lives were being changed. There was power in it. I came back home that night and thought, "*I didn't curse all day. This is a miracle. And I didn't get angry all day.*" I believe God took those two things from me. I think He took the anger because I would've ended up dead.

KATHIE LEE: Or somebody else would've been.

ROGER: He just took the anger. At the same time, He took cursing out of my mouth. I had used its quota of curse words for a whole life. He said, "*You're done. That's it. You've used it up.*"

From that point on, I went to Calvary Chapel Costa Mesa. I was playing professionally as a bass player at that time. This music was exploding in Calvary Chapel Costa Mesa, which was the epicenter of the Jesus Movement, with all these bands. I showed up and got introduced to some of the musicians, and there weren't enough bass players. As we started to fellowship, they realized I had a pretty deep knowledge of the Bible. I even answered some of their questions.

So they thought I'd been a Christian a long time, when in fact it had been just months. They just threw me in. All of a sudden, I was playing worship with a worship band. Now I was on a mission. My first two years as a Christian, I'd just beat atheist heads into the concrete over and over, which won arguments but didn't make other fellow believers. Then I realized, "*Wait a minute—*"

KATHIE LEE: Do I want to be right or righteous?

ROGER: You can be so right, you're wrong. To make a long story short, that is my journey into Christianity and into knowing God.

KATHIE LEE: In all the ensuing years, has there ever been a crisis of faith? I know you've had a health issue and a marriage that didn't work. We all have drama in our lives. In this world, we will have trouble, Jesus said. So, did you have a crisis of faith, anywhere along the way, about what you had decided about the Bible or about Jesus? Or was that decisive for you?

ROGER: It was decisive. There has never been a moment when I doubted God. The Bible is true no matter what anybody says, and I can just go right down the line with anybody who is logical and show them there is no other choice. It doesn't matter what you want, it doesn't matter what you feel, the Bible is true. End of story. There is no other option, logically.

KATHIE LEE: But do you want to follow it? That's a whole other thing. Thank you so much for sharing your story with us, Roger.

TWENTY

SOMETHING GREATER THAN OURSELVES

LISA KITTREDGE

Mike Kittredge was one of those larger-than-life individuals who created something out of nothing and made us wonder, *Why didn't I think of that?* Mike founded Yankee Candle fifty-two years ago in Holyoke, Massachusetts, in his garage, where he made candles for his mother's friends. But not just your average candle. He introduced fragrances that released as the candle burned, creating a new sensory experience to an ancient craft. Genius. Mike had significant personal and physical challenges along the way, marital woes and several bouts with cancer, until one day he decided to sell his company and build the world's most beautiful private yacht. Oh yes, and marry the young woman who had seen him through his cancer.

That was Lisa, who started as an employee and began to share something much deeper with this brilliant but complicated man she worked for. Our families met on the glorious island of Nantucket, and we spent many years traveling the world together on their boat, *Paraffin*.

One night, at one of their legendary dinners in Nantucket, the question was asked of all the guests: "If you could have dinner with anyone in history, who would it be?" To my surprise (because Mike adored the Beatles), he replied, "Jesus." Later, I asked him, "Why Jesus?" Mike said, "If He is who He says He is, then it changes everything."

Mike suffered a major, life-threatening stroke in 2012. Although he and Lisa were separated at the time and in the process of a divorce, Lisa saved his life by getting him to the hospital in Boston in time for treatment. While he was recuperating from brain surgery, I was privileged to pray with Mike to receive Jesus into his heart. Sadly, he passed away in 2019. Let's hear their story now, with Lisa, two years after Mike's death.

KATHIE LEE: So, Lisa, tell me about the family you grew up in. Was it a religious home?

LISA: My mom and dad were both raised Catholic. So we went to church every Sunday. We were baptized, we received First Communion, we were confirmed.

KATHIE LEE: Meaning you and your brother and sister.

LISA: Yes, I had two brothers and a sister. My dad worked all the time to make sure there was food on the table. I think my mom became disillusioned with the Catholic religion and moved away from it. As we got older, we didn't enjoy it. But I'm very much at peace with how I consider whatever my faith is now. It's not a specific faith. I definitely believe that there's a greater something overseeing us and guiding us and keeping us on track, whether it's Jesus or God or Buddha or Allah. I don't know. I'm not particularly convinced who it is, and I'm not sure it matters. What I think matters is that we all know that there's something greater than ourselves.

KATHIE LEE: Tell me about meeting Mike and how that changed your life.

LISA: Well, it changed my life dramatically. When I first met him, I was a senior in college. I just worked for him at that point. As time went on,

I started moving up in the company, and we spent more time together. I was intrigued with his incredible mind and his creativity, and I was so excited to have the opportunity to learn from him. I loved talking to him. In hindsight, you know, he was my boss, so there was something there that was totally inappropriate. I wasn't in love with him right away. I was intrigued, I was fascinated, and then I totally fell in love with him. I can remember thinking, "*Oh, maybe this is the way it's supposed to be.*" He was so into me.

KATHIE LEE: And let's be honest, it was flattering. He wanted you.

LISA: I came from a middle-class family. I was able to do regular things but not travel a lot, so that was exciting. Within a year of dating, he was diagnosed with Hodgkin's. Our entire relationship changed. I'm not the type of person to abandon someone I care about.

KATHIE LEE: Were you in love with him when he got diagnosed?

LISA: Yes. I was in love with him. I had committed to being in a relationship with him. And I was a part of his son Mick's life at that point.

KATHIE LEE: Remember that time we sat around that beautiful table in Nantucket, and I asked, "If you could have dinner with anyone in history, who would it be?" Mike said, "Jesus." And I asked him later, "Why Jesus?" He said, "If He is who He says He is, then it changes everything." And the time I came up to the hospital after his stroke, he asked for forgiveness for what he'd done to you and asked Jesus into his heart. He used to say, "My soul is still my soul."

LISA: He would recite the prayers he learned as a child. He was raised Catholic too. He would recite the Our Father and Hail Mary.

KATHIE LEE: Tell me about the night that the stroke happened.

LISA: Our marriage was ending. I had moved from the main house to the guesthouse. I told him, "I can't do this anymore. Let's get through the holidays, and then we'll go from there."

So I was at the guesthouse, and I had a meeting that morning at the girls' school. Mike used to come down in the morning and kiss the girls goodbye, and I would take them to school. He had just had shoulder surgery, so he couldn't drive. I got a call from the main house that Mike wasn't feeling well, so he wasn't going to come down. I said okay and took the kids to school. I came back and took a shower and got ready for my meeting.

Then I received a text from the house saying, "Something's going on with Mike." I went up to the house and saw Mike in the guest-room bed, and he couldn't speak. I screamed for someone to call an ambulance. Thankfully, someone already had.

KATHIE LEE: So you went to the hospital?

LISA: Our little hospital knew right away it was not something they could handle, so they put him in an ambulance and sent him to Brigham. My brother, Marc, drove me. Mike was admitted. I went in to say good night to him. He told me he loved me and held my hand.

KATHIE LEE: So he could still speak then?

LISA: Basically, that's all he could say. And then the next morning I went in superearly because I couldn't sleep. They said his prognosis was not good. I couldn't comprehend that Mike wasn't going to be able to get through another medical challenge. So many surgeries, so many cancer treatments, the heart surgery. There was just so much that he'd been able to get through. They basically told me how the rest of his life was going to be. I couldn't comprehend that was true.

KATHIE LEE: So what was going on with your girls at that point?

LISA: Well, I didn't let them see him for two weeks. Finally, when they could sit him up in a chair, the nurses covered up the equipment and said it was okay for the girls to see him. I mean, they were so young.

KATHIE LEE: How old were they at the time?

LISA: Kylie had just turned nine, and Casey was six. It was really, really hard to see their dad like that. Thank God I had help that I felt okay leaving them with, to be with him.

KATHIE LEE: You knew the road you were on was separation and then likely divorce. Now were you thinking, "*I'm going to take care of this man for the rest of my life*"?

LISA: Honestly, I wasn't thinking that far ahead. I knew I had to change the whole house. I had to put ramps in and change bathrooms. He had the stroke in November. And it took until March. I had lots of help, thank God, but I was in charge.

KATHIE LEE: Okay, so let's fast-forward. We'll just say, ultimately, it did end in divorce. So life goes on. So when you went to Israel, tell me why you wanted to go?

LISA: Well, you and Frank had asked Mike and I to go a year or two prior, but there was some political stuff going on over there, and Mike didn't want to go.

KATHIE LEE: And I told him what I tell everybody, "I've been going to Israel since I was seventeen years old, and I was told even then that it's not a good time." It's always going to be dangerous in the eyes of the world because of bad information. But you love to travel.

LISA: Oh, I love to explore new areas. I love to learn. And you talked so much about it, I was really excited. I did want to go. And I loved it far more than I thought I would.

KATHIE LEE: Tell me about that.

LISA: There's two particular instances that blew me away. You know Herod's . . . way up high on a cliff.

KATHIE LEE: Masada?

LISA: Yes. That was just mind-boggling to me. And the other experience was Bethlehem. I, in my mind, had this vision of what Bethlehem was, thinking it was so romantic and mystical because that's where Jesus was born. And then when we went, it was in the Palestinian region. It was a completely different experience for me.

KATHIE LEE: It's one of my least favorite places.

LISA: You know, all the stories and scriptures make me think. One of the things I wanted to say to you today is that I think we all have a belief system . . . Christianity, I guess. There are stories to support that belief. And you're going to continually look for those stories. It's just fascinating to me. And it's such a historical place, going there and seeing those places. Even the Dead Sea Scrolls—something new was going on with them when we were there.

KATHIE LEE: Yes. You can't imagine the stuff they've discovered since we've been there. Every day there is affirmation. It's all just lining up: Solomon, David, the money changers. They were written thousands of years ago, but they happened. It goes back to what Mike said: "If He is who He says He is, then it changes everything."

Now, you grew up having Jesus defined to you by the Catholic Church. What changed about the person of Jesus for you in Israel, from what you had learned in the Catholic Church? I mean, from your experience growing up in a religion as opposed to finding out about Jesus the Man, the living, breathing Jew?

LISA: Yeah. I wasn't brought up with that information. I think it opens your mind to possibilities. I think the bigger picture is that whatever the story is, whoever He was, He was here to teach us something. There's good and bad, right and wrong; most of us know what the difference is, but sometimes we need guidance. We're all in this together. We all have pain. If we can just listen and stop trying to be so righteous, I think that's what God or Jesus is trying to teach. At the time that those Scriptures were written, there were reasons, there were miracles that happened to save people. So I don't know how much my interpretation of what Jesus was meant to be for me or the world changed. I think it just opened up the possibilities of "That's an interesting way to look at it" or "That's different from the way I was brought up" or "I didn't know that."

KATHIE LEE: I know you stopped taking Communion because you were deeply hurt at how the church treated your mother about the divorce from your father.

LISA: My mom was in a situation that she knew she was going to have to get out of, and that's why, after Marc was born, she went back to school. She knew she was going to have to take care of herself and her children. And she did. She got a degree and started a career in speech pathology, and she still practices it today. So now she's completely disgusted with the Catholic Church. I still think she believes in God though.

I don't often pray. I meditate, and if I do pray, it's typically when

I'm scared or overwhelmed with joy and gratitude. On a daily basis, I try to practice some form of meditation because I know I need to center myself some days more than others. I do that through breathing and mantras that I've learned over the years. In some ways, I feel like praying is a mantra.

KATHIE LEE: Yes, well, it's the living, breathing Word of God. Tell me, I know you didn't get baptized in the Jordan River when we were there. Why not?

LISA: Because I felt like I had been baptized, so if the idea was to get rid of my original sin, then didn't I already do that? It felt uncomfortable to me at the time. I considered it, but I didn't feel like I would've been authentic by jumping in and doing it.

KATHIE LEE: That's why I wanted this group of people there. I knew everyone would respond differently, and I was fascinated to see it unfold. I wanted to create an environment where everyone felt safe to express what they were feeling. At the Garden of Gethsemane, you took Communion for the first time in years. Why?

LISA: One of the reasons you can't take Communion at church is because you haven't been to confession or you haven't done what you're supposed to do. So I felt like at that point I had been a pretty good girl, and it felt like that was okay to me.

KATHIE LEE: How did you feel when you did it?

LISA: It felt familiar. I can't say there was any dramatic shift in me or anything. Maybe if you want to put it in the words of what the lesson is, it's "He's going to accept us no matter where we're at or who we are and help us"—whoever "He" is, whether it's Jesus or God or you know. He's going to accept you no matter what.

KATHIE LEE: How different is it taking Communion in the Garden of Gethsemane, where Jesus spent His last night before being crucified? Did the weightiness of that impact you?

LISA: Absolutely it did. There's no question. Like you were in a different world. That was powerful.

KATHIE LEE: Would you go back?

LISA: Absolutely.

KATHIE LEE: You just have to keep learning. I think it's worth having another trip with as many people from our last trip. Everyone bring more of their family.

LISA: I would love that.

KATHIE LEE: Well, I love you for sharing, Lisa.

TWENTY-ONE

THE RELUCTANT PROPHET

HUBIE SYNN

To meet him, you would get the impression that Hubie is a mild-mannered, quiet, hardworking certified public accountant living in the New Jersey suburbs with his wife and five children. And while all this is true, it is merely a small piece of the puzzle that is Hubie.

Think of a supernatural superhero, and Hubie is Clark Kent. He has gifts that belie his appearance—gifts of the Spirit, as they are called in the Scripture. As 1 Corinthians 12:4 says, "There are different kinds of gifts, but the same Spirit distributes them." The Holy Spirit is given to each believer in a special way: To some people, the Spirit gives a message of knowledge. To others, He gives the gift of faith, healing, the power to do miracles, the ability to prophesy . . . and more. He gives gifts to each person, just as He decides.

Many people have trouble believing that God still gives these gifts to His followers today. But Jesus said in John 14:12, "Whoever believes in me will do the works I have been doing, and they will do even greater things than these, because I am going to the Father."

Meet the dear friend I call "the reluctant prophet." You will love Hubie Synn.

KATHIE LEE: Hubie, tell me, did you grow up in a faith family?

HUBIE: My mother didn't really have a lot of education. But she would read the Bible and act on it. That was one thing about my mother I really admired.

KATHIE LEE: What about your dad?

HUBIE: Well, my dad didn't really want anything to do with it. My mother dragged us to church because she was into the Catholic faith because of my grandmother. We went to CCD classes, First Communion, confirmation, stuff like that. So my mother was into that, and my dad wasn't. My dad would go only on a special occasion.

KATHIE LEE: So when did you become a Christian?

HUBIE: I kind of grew up with it, so it planted its seeds. I used to make fun of my mother because she watched a televangelist and sent him money. But when my wife, Vicki, and I had a bad car accident, and we realized that we both should have died, that kind of woke me up. I started going to different churches because I was like, "*If you should have died and you didn't, then obviously you must have some kind of reason for living.*"

KATHIE LEE: God must have a purpose for you.

HUBIE: Exactly. We found a Methodist church that was near us. We started to go there and meet people, and that kind of got us started back on the road.

KATHIE LEE: Okay, all right. You're starting along this path and you're back to church, and then you have your children and you're making a living as an accountant, is that true?

HUBIE: Yes, I am a CPA. I had my own practice in Manhattan, and Vicki was working at a consumer products company. We were both working and just living life and thinking, "*We go to church on Sundays, and everything is good.*" Vicki joined the music ministry, and I got thrown into the kids' church.

KATHIE LEE: I've always affectionately described you as "the reluctant prophet." Tell me how God led you into this whole new dimension. First of all, what is it you now do that is so unique?

HUBIE: As time went on, I felt these impulses. It's like when something just drops into your spirit, or you just have an idea, and you're like, "Where'd that come from?" They started coming more often, and I started to go up to people, tap them on the shoulder, and say, "Hey, by the way, God wants you to know this . . . ," and then I would leave.

KATHIE LEE: Were you at that time reluctant? Because a lot of people don't want a stranger to come up to them and say anything.

HUBIE: Actually, I was very reluctant. But these thoughts just kept coming; they wouldn't stop. I just decided, "*You know what? I'll just go. I'll look like an idiot once, and then I can say at least I tested it out.*"

KATHIE LEE: Right.

HUBIE: That didn't happen. It had a different reaction.

KATHIE LEE: What did most people say?

HUBIE: Most people would look at me like, "Who are you? Are you an angel?" I would crack up and say, "Well, my last name is Synn, so that's out of the question." They wanted to know more about me, but I would just try to get away because it felt uncomfortable to me.

KATHIE LEE: Right.

HUBIE: Some of them were calling me God's earpiece, God's mind, and those are pretty big words. I'm as messed up as everybody else. We're all struggling to get through this life. The reluctant thing came because if I got the impulse, it would build up over time. And if I didn't do anything, I would get sick. God would start to highlight people to me in public places: restaurants, out on the street, gas stations, all these places. I just started to tap people and tell them very quickly, "God says this . . . ," and I would just leave. A lot of them wanted to come after me to find out who I was.

KATHIE LEE: Were you only telling them good things? I mean, sometimes a word can be a cautionary thing. What were these first messages like in nature?

HUBIE: Some of them were, "You're having a difficult time, and God wants you to know very shortly this is going to change," or "God knows you've been waiting a long time for something, and you think He's not hearing you." Things like that. They were very detailed, and people were like, "How did you know this?"

KATHIE LEE: But they were words of encouragement, basically.

HUBIE: Yeah.

KATHIE LEE: Well, everybody needs that. So when did it start to change and become what would appear to be the miraculous?

HUBIE: After a while, when people started to look at me differently, it was a very hard thing for me to deal with because I felt like I was losing my identity. I wasn't Hubie anymore; I was the man of God, the oracle of God. Those were such high names that it was scary to me. Then when people run up to you so you can pray for them, it puts pressure on you.

KATHIE LEE: Well, yeah, I understand. A lot of people go to mediums or to psychics because they want to know the future. But explain to us the difference—people cannot go to you and say, "Give me a word," right?

HUBIE: When you seek a prophetic person out, they're supposed to only give you a word when God gives them something. Unfortunately, I know quite a few who just give a word to somebody whenever they want it, which isn't necessarily in my mind the right way to do it.

KATHIE LEE: It makes them feel important.

HUBIE: Right. I mean, if you're really seeking God, He'll find you wherever you are. It kind of took a toll on me because I felt like people just wanted to use me all the time.

KATHIE LEE: They wanted something from you.

HUBIE: Right. David Tyree once told me, "Hubie, everybody values your gift but not you, and you need to come to terms with that." So I spent time with the Lord, like, "*You need to help me get through this situation because I'm not feeling like myself.*" Then the Lord spoke to me, "*You have My gift, but it's Mine, not yours. And if you are My workman, you use it when I tell you to use it, and don't use it any other time.*"

KATHIE LEE: How do you know David Tyree?

HUBIE: Right. I went to work for a financial person, and we did his finances. We had a meeting at his house, and that's where I first met him.

KATHIE LEE: Okay.

HUBIE: We went back to the office, and the Lord kept badgering me to pray for this man. That happened over a couple of weeks, and it wouldn't stop. The Lord said, "*You need to call him.*" Finally, I said, "*Okay, Lord, I'm going to do this.*" I went to work, I went through the Rolodex, and I made a copy of David's number. Then I went home—it was a Friday—because I figured, thinking the worst-case scenario, "*If something blows up, I have the weekend to deal with this.*"

KATHIE LEE: Get a backup plan.

HUBIE: Yeah, exactly. I called him Friday night, like seven o'clock. He picked up and said, "Hi, this is David." And I froze. I didn't know what to say. I said, "Hi, it's Hubie." He was like, "Who?" I said, "Hubie, the guy who's going to do your taxes." And he was like, "Yeah, okay, how're you doing, man?" I said, "Okay." So it was quiet. He was probably thinking, "*Why are you calling me?*" and I couldn't talk. I was like, "*Lord, You want me to speak to him, but nothing's coming out. There's a problem.*"

KATHIE LEE: A little awkward on a Friday night at seven o'clock!

HUBIE: Exactly. Then all of a sudden, I just went, "David, God wants to tell you . . . ," and it came out.

KATHIE LEE: Exactly what did God want him to know?

HUBIE: God wanted him to know that He was going to put him in the spotlight. He was going to have a platform to share the gospel. He would be known as a wide receiver, and his life was going to change dramatically—something along those lines.

KATHIE LEE: Right.

HUBIE: Then after I finished, it was like an eerie quiet. I went, "*This guy must think I'm a lunatic.*" He said, "You know, a lot of things you said, my wife and I were just praying about." And I went, "*Thank God.*" He said, "I want to get to know you a little more." So I gave him my phone number and went to visit him a couple of times. That was back in October when he was injured; he wasn't even playing. Then the Super

Bowl was four months later, and when he made that catch, all those things came true.

KATHIE LEE: He made one of the most iconic catches in Super Bowl history, right?

HUBIE: Yes, one of the greatest plays in Super Bowl history. David called me the next morning, and he said, "Can you believe what Jesus did?" I said, "I can't." He said, "I'm going to tell everybody about you." And I went, "No, please don't do that. I want no credit for this. God did what He did." At the beginning, he would say "a friend." Then *Charisma* magazine did a full spread on him, and they mentioned me. All of a sudden, my name, Hubie Synn, started to go out. Then David wrote a book and put me in there. This thing started to take on a life of its own, and I couldn't stop it. People looked at me differently; they would say, "The prophet is here." It was a weird type of situation, and I had to deal with this identity issue.

KATHIE LEE: You were a curiosity object.

HUBIE: Right. People automatically want to be my friend; they want to hang out, but they didn't want anything to do with me before. During that time, I kind of worked out my issues.

KATHIE LEE: Tell me about your encounter with Jonathan Cahn. You were at the airport, and you saw a man you did not recognize. Tell me about that.

HUBIE: I was at the airport in Charlotte, trying to get to Dallas. Everything was getting canceled. And all of a sudden, the Lord placed on my heart, "*See that man over there? Go and give him a word.*" I didn't want to. I was exhausted. I just wanted to get to Dallas. But if I don't give the word, I start to get sick.

KATHIE LEE: Anyway, you went on to tell this man, Jonathan Cahn, that he had something, and you didn't know what it was, but it was the manuscript for *The Harbinger*. Am I right?

HUBIE: Yes.

KATHIE LEE: And what did you tell him was going to happen?

HUBIE: It was something about God gave him this book, and God was going to bring the right people to help get it out. It was going to go all over the world and change his life dramatically. It was very detailed. And over the subsequent years, this came true. *The Harbinger*, when it came out, it went on the *New York Times* bestseller list, and it stayed there for a very long time.

KATHIE LEE: Okay, so later, I got a message from dear friends SQuire Rushnell and his wife, Louise DuArt, that you had a message for me. Tell me about that.

HUBIE: Yes, SQuire and Louise said they were going to go have lunch with you. All of a sudden, the Lord was like, "*You need to send her a message.*" I thought, "*No, I don't want to do this.*" Finally, the Lord was like, "*You really need to do this*," and then I started getting sick. So I started typing this message to you, and my hands were shaking. I didn't know how you'd react. Then I got word back that it helped you and that you were very open to it.

KATHIE LEE: Yes, and as I remember, you told me that somebody was coming against me, but God was going to overcome, and it was all going to be reconciled. It turned out the person coming against me was Howard Stern, and yes, it was reconciled. I prayed for that man every single day. Then thirty years later, he asked me for forgiveness. Some of these things take a long, long time! You and I became friends through that, and the Lord gave you words of tremendous encouragement. Every single thing you have said to me over the last five or six years has come true. And you always say at the end of your message, "But it's not going to be what you think." We have to be careful in the interpretation of these words, too, don't we?

HUBIE: Yes, I have learned that when I get a word, I just kind of walk down the path. I don't know the timeline. I've learned just to kind of live my life, and then I just see what happens.

KATHIE LEE: Well, this is really fascinating. Why are so many people—and they're wonderful followers of Jesus—why are they afraid to go deeper into the gifts of the spirit world? A lot of people believe in all the miracles Jesus did, they believe in all the miracles in the Bible, but they don't believe miracles happen that way anymore, even though Scripture is very clear. Jesus Himself said, "Greater things than I have done you will do in My name." Jesus is the same yesterday, today, and forever. If Jesus healed, and He told His followers that we would heal, why are we afraid when we heal in the name of Jesus? It's not we who are doing the healing; we are facilitating the work of the Holy Spirit—am I wrong?

HUBIE: No, you're right. I think the reason that it's not more accepted is because, at one point, it was commercialized. You see some of the televangelists—not that I'm picking on them because that's what kind of brought me back. But I think that when people make it sensationalized—

KATHIE LEE: Or take money for it.

HUBIE: Right, with the number on the screen and whatever, I think people get turned off. I know I did.

KATHIE LEE: Yeah.

HUBIE: I don't ask for anything, as you know. I just do what I do, and God will take care of whatever my needs are.

KATHIE LEE: God takes care of you because you happen to be a heck of an accountant!

HUBIE: Exactly. But I think that's part of it. And I think that in the United States, you can just most of the time buy whatever you want.

KATHIE LEE: Right.

HUBIE: When you're in need, you really start looking for God.

KATHIE LEE: Yeah, and you'd give your last penny for a miracle, wouldn't you? There are lots of reasons we run to God, and many of them are out of desperation, I would say.

HUBIE: Yes. But if something doesn't go right for people, they blame God—and that bothers me. Then one day, God was like, "*I don't need you to protect Me.*" When God does His miracles, He's showing people that, in real life, He still exists.

KATHIE LEE: He loves us.

HUBIE: Yes.

KATHIE LEE: Hubie, what does Jesus look like to you now as opposed to when you were younger?

HUBIE: I was a very bad control freak at one time. But when you realize you're not in control, when you have no control over certain things, like your kids get sick, or you have a strained relationship and you can't fix it, it's very frustrating. The Jesus I serve, I know that no matter what, He's with me, and He's going to help me through it. I really don't have to worry too much about issues. They may be difficult, but, ultimately, I'm going to be victorious.

KATHIE LEE: Well, I love you, Hubie, and I love your story because it is a very unique one. Thank you for the great friend you've been to me.

TWENTY-TWO

NOTHING IS IMPOSSIBLE WITH GOD

JOANNE MOODY

I have met with a lot of faith leaders during my decades of ministry all over the world. I came to faith through Billy Graham's ministry and was blessed to become his friend. In my early twenties, I attended Oral Roberts University for two and a half years and performed with his television program the entire time.

When I moved to LA to continue my career after college, my first job was being the singer on the world-famous evangelist Kathryn Kuhlman's television show, *I Believe in Miracles*. I have seen up close and personal almost all the well-known personalities in the faith world and have witnessed a lot of behavior I wish I'd never seen. But I have also met some of the most incredible, godly, righteous, and genuine followers of Jesus who exist on this planet.

Joanne Moody is one of them. She has become a close confidante and personal friend. I have shared my darkest secrets with her, as she powerfully led me through some desperately needed inner healing. And yet she is as easy to share a gut-level laugh with as anyone in entertainment. Like me, she doesn't separate the spiritual from the secular. She just authentically lives her abundant, extraordinary, amazing life in Jesus every day. Her story is truly miraculous.

KATHIE LEE: Joanne, I've never heard any story like yours. Can you start with the faith nature of your family? Were you a God-believing family?

JOANNE: Yeah, my family grew up Catholic. In those days, the Catholic Church was quite different than today. I didn't know God was a loving Father. I knew He was God, and I knew Jesus was my Lord and Savior. I went through all the Catholic stuff until I was about thirteen; my family sort of fell away from churchgoing. I really didn't ever lose this idea that God is who He says He is, that Jesus is the Son, but me having intimacy with God? No, that came a long time later.

KATHIE LEE: Okay, well, then, I know you had two separate careers. You were very active in the music world, and you were very active in the athletic world.

JOANNE: Yes. I left home at seventeen. I couldn't live under my father's rules anymore. I started taking classes at the University of Hawaii; I wanted to do music as a career. But I also started running, and I became a maniac about individual sports, running, weight training. I decided to go to school for that at the American College of Sports Medicine.

KATHIE LEE: Smart, smart.

JOANNE: I did school for both those things, but I ran up against the wall with music because the university only wanted opera. And I was doing R & B and pop, singing in bands. So I left that school and focused on writing and recording albums and then continuing with exercise science. Over the next twenty-three years, that's what I did.

KATHIE LEE: Had you met Mike, your husband, at that time?

JOANNE: I had not. I was married to a man named Kevin during those years and got divorced when I was thirty-one.

KATHIE LEE: Was that a heartbreaker for you?

JOANNE: Interestingly, that led me back to the Lord because I was wandering around, studying everything from New Age to Buddhism to Taoism. I studied everything there was to study. It was fascinating to me. Anyway, I met Mike when I was thirty-four. We got married a couple of years later. I got saved when I was dating him, had this crazy salvation story.

KATHIE LEE: What happened?

JOANNE: I was in a really bad situation, and that took a toll on my health. I was having all kinds of issues. And then I lost my voice, which was the biggest scare of my life at that time. I was on the radio singing all the time, and I lost my voice.

KATHIE LEE: Yeah, because it defines you. When you lose something like that, you say, "Who am I if I don't have that?"

JOANNE: It was not only my identity, but it was my livelihood.

KATHIE LEE: Okay, so you lost your voice, and then what happened?

JOANNE: There was a cyst on my vocal cords, and they were going to have to do surgery. I'd had a cyst four years before that my surgeon removed without any issue, and I had a three-octave range at that time.

KATHIE LEE: Wow!

JOANNE: But he said to me something that freaked me out: "Jo, I don't want to do that surgery again on you because I believe this time it's going to scar, and you'll lose your upper register." And I went, "No, I can't do that." So on top of all this stuff, I can't sing, I can't be on the radio.

KATHIE LEE: I hate it. Yeah, I've been through it.

JOANNE: And on the way back home, I just started crying, remembering I had a bottle of sleeping pills at home. As I was driving down on the freeway, I said, "I'm going to kill myself when I get home," which is so strange if you know me. I'm optimism to the tenth power.

KATHIE LEE: Oh yeah, now you are!

JOANNE: Right, but I had hit the bottom. I yelled at God, "What did I ever do to You that You would hate me so much?" I said, "If You were even real, You would show me." And in a split second, this flattop white VW van swerved in front of me and almost knocked my bumper off. I mean, it just jolted me.

KATHIE LEE: Yeah.

JOANNE: And the license plate said DEUT 6:5. I was like, "*Is that a Bible verse? That's so weird.*" I pulled up to my driveway of my little Quonset hut rental house. I was shaking inside and thinking, "*Okay, if that was God, and this 'DEUT 6:5' means something, then I can't kill myself. I've got to figure out what I'm going to do next.*" Eventually I got a Bible, opened it up to the index. I opened up Deuteronomy 6:5, and the scripture is "Love the Lord your God with all your heart and with all your soul and with all your strength." And I thought, "*I've never done that.*" And I fell on my knees and said, "God, I'm so sorry. All I cared about was doing my own thing. I have never loved You with all this. I'm so sorry." And the power of Jesus fell on me. And I sobbed and sobbed. I was just wrecked from the inside out.

Thankfully the cyst burst, and then I had no problems with my voice. My throat was still really tender, and I couldn't go right back to singing, but I did not need surgery.

Then I went to LA to a conference. A woman was prophesying, and she called me out in the back of the room. I was so freaked out. I was still a recovering Catholic. She said, "You in the back, right there." I was looking around like, "*She can't be pointing to me because I'm certainly not going up there.*" And she said, "Come here." And the power of God started falling on me. I was shaking, and I couldn't control myself. I got all the way up to the front, and she said, "You came from the islands, you sing, and you write, and that's your life. But your life is going to be to heal the sick, to cast out demons, and to raise the dead." She put her hand up, and the power of God smacked me, and I fell down. All I could think of in my logical mind was "*I've got to get out of here. These people are flipping nuts,*" but I couldn't move. It's like I was under the weightiness of God, and I was being taken up and being shown Jesus on His throne in glory. And I was thinking, "*Jo Moody, snap out of it. You're crazy.*" I was between logic and the supernatural. And finally, this lifted off me, and I was still shaking.

KATHIE LEE: So did anybody explain to you what was happening to you?

JOANNE: Yeah. Fortunately there were pastors who explained to me what happened. And then I just dove in, deep dive with the Lord. I just wanted to know Him.

KATHIE LEE: How long did that period last before God led you to the fulfillment of that woman's prophecy?

JOANNE: Yeah, such a great question—almost twenty-four years.

KATHIE LEE: Wow! He's The God of the How and When.

JOANNE: Exactly. A couple of years later, I had a similar prophecy. Only this was when I was about seven months pregnant with my son. I was leading worship at this conference. A prophetic woman said, "You're marked by God." I was thinking, "*Oh, that's good because all I want to do is music for the Lord.*" That was my narrow-minded human thought.

KATHIE LEE: Yeah, we put God in a box.

JOANNE: She said, "You're marked by God for this greatness on your life." She said, "I don't even know what this word is, but I can see it over you. Do you know the word *Lipizzan*?" And I said, "Yes, those are my favorite horses." And she said, "That's how the Lord views you. You are a Lipizzan stallion, but you are wild. So the Lord is going to allow your legs to be broken. And He's going to put you in a stall, and He's going to feed you. And then after a time, everything will be restored to you, and you will burst out of the barn, and you will lead nations." I was thinking because I was pregnant and superuncomfortable, that was the breaking of my legs. I seriously did. I was that naive.

KATHIE LEE: No, that's water. Your water breaks, not your legs!

JOANNE: So stinking funny, yes, who knew then. I put that prophecy away, and I gave birth to my son. I went through a ninety-one-hour nonprogressive labor, fried the nerves and my pelvis, went through fourteen and a half years and thirteen surgeries, and a near-death experience, never thinking about that prophetic word. Then seven years later, I went in my closet, and it fell out of a journal that fell off my shelf.

KATHIE LEE: The prophecy. Wow!

JOANNE: Fell off the shelf in year seven of my affliction.

KATHIE LEE: You just went through all that litany of things that happened to you. Basically, you were in excruciating pain.

JOANNE: Yes, paralyzed with pain. By year five, I was on seven different narcotics.

KATHIE LEE: What happened to your faith during all that?

JOANNE: I was weirdly holding on to Jesus with everything in my being. I was in so much pain, the only thing I could do was hang on to God for dear life.

KATHIE LEE: Praise God.

JOANNE: Yeah, I think overall, I learned things about the Lord during those suffering years. I believe that sometimes when the enemy comes at us, and we do have suffering, the Lord works it together for good—Romans 8:28—because we are called according to His purposes. I don't subscribe to the theology that there's some additional redemption in suffering because then Jesus didn't pay at all. But Jesus did pay it all.

KATHIE LEE: Good point. Yes, but He does say He will take your ashes and bring beauty from it. So tell me, you went through fourteen and a half years since the tragedy in that delivery room. What happened to you on the day God delivered you?

JOANNE: Rarely in your life you hear an audible voice of God, but I did in April 2013. I was facing my fourteenth surgery. I thought, "*What are You asking of me, God?*" I got in the elevator at Stanford University Medical Center, and I felt the intensity of God on me. And I heard this: "*Contend for your healing.*" And I was thinking, "*What?*"

About a week later, I heard again the audible voice of God saying to me, "*Go to Voice of the Apostles. You'll be blessed.*" I googled it, and Voice of the Apostles was a conference in Orlando, Florida. I said to God, "Why would You say that to me? You know I can't fly. I can't sit. How am I going to go to that?" And then I just felt His presence. I called my friend Michelle, and I said, "Hey, I heard the audible voice of God, and this is what He said." And she said, "Oh, fantastic, you're going to get healed there." She's one of those people who has the gift of faith.

KATHIE LEE: It's such a beautiful thing.

JOANNE: But the thought of having to be in excruciating pain and trapped in an airplane, I couldn't. I called my doctor, who said, "Look, Jo, I'm going to write to the airline, and you will only have to sit to take off and land. Otherwise, you can be on your knees." So I rode on a plane from Sacramento to Orlando on a pillow, on my knees. And when I got there, I encountered the Holy Spirit in a way I never had before. I was just absolutely knocked out under the glory of God. And from the moment when I came up from that experience with the Lord, I knew so many things about people's lives. It was like a veil had been removed from me.

KATHIE LEE: What would you call that?

JOANNE: I think it was a gift from the Lord for my life. But I didn't get healed when that happened. I was disappointed, but not disappointed in God because the word from Him was, "*You'll be blessed.*" I did feel blessed. I am that kind of person anyway, even as rough as all those years were.

KATHIE LEE: Yeah, you're a half-full girl.

JOANNE: Yeah. But just before the conference ended, a man asked me what my story was. I didn't want any more people to pray for me and to be disappointed anymore. I just said, "I'm a chronic pain patient, and I've been like this almost fifteen years. It's okay." And he was like, "Well, could I pray for you?" And I put out my hands, like, "*Get it over with,*" not that I didn't have faith to be healed, but I didn't in that moment.

KATHIE LEE: Yeah, who could blame you?

JOANNE: Our God came over me, and I wasn't healed again. Twenty-five minutes later, the man came back. His name tag said "Richard." I said, "Richard, thanks for praying for me. It didn't work, but it's fine. I've been this way a really long time." Then he yelled, "No! God healed me, He healed my son of cancer, and now He's going to heal you!" And this man took me through the breaking of all the lies I believed about God, that even though I loved God, He really didn't want to heal me, that I wasn't trustworthy. And on and on, with even my anger toward God, the things I buried so deep, he brought all those things up. And in the light of the Holy Spirit, in the light of Jesus' love, I got healed of all that.

And then he commanded every oppressing spirit that was harassing me to leave. And then the last thing he did was pray for my pelvic pain and my nerves to be restored. And in a moment, all the pain left. Makes no sense medically. I am a medical miracle.

KATHIE LEE: Yes, I've seen it. From that moment on, what healing work did God lead you to?

JOANNE: It was like being shot out of a cannon. I had this experience that Jesus' gift of healing by His blood was given to every believer. It had never dawned on me that's what we were supposed to be doing.

KATHIE LEE: In fact, He said, greater things they will do in My name.

JOANNE: And from the moment I got back, I started doing what I had been experiencing at Voice of the Apostles. God told me to start a non-profit, told me what to call it, gave me this mandate: "*I want you to go and do the greater things, and I want you to raise up an army called the Kingdom Family to do it with you, and they're going to surpass you, and they're going to be here long after you. And you will never again in your lifetime see a move like what I'm about to do.*" He told me that in October 2013. I went to online theology school, and I did everything He told me to do. My testimony went out like wildfire.

KATHIE LEE: Wow! So to wrap up the message of this faith journey, which is far from over, at this point, what is it today? What is the miracle of your life? How would you describe it?

JOANNE: The miracle of my life is Jesus—God of the impossible. Nothing is impossible with God—physical healing, emotional healing, spiritual healing. And for those who believe, there is a destiny greater than you could ever hope, imagine, dream, or think, and it's already done for you. He already made a way. He said, "*Just believe Me, and step into it.*"

TWENTY-THREE

FINDING THE JESUS WHO FORGIVES

VICKI GIFFORD KENNEDY

In 1981, my husband Frank's daughter, Vicki, married Michael Kennedy, the sixth child of Robert and Ethel Kennedy. They brought three beautiful children into the world before Michael tragically died in a skiing accident in Aspen, Colorado, on New Year's Eve 1997. Sadly, they were in the midst of a divorce at the time.

Today Vicki is a vibrant, beautiful woman deeply connected to her children and grandchildren and immersed in living a beautiful, purposeful life. But it has been a struggle for her since her childhood. Most people are familiar with her father, of course, the legendary football player and sportscaster Frank Gifford. But few would be familiar with Vicki's mother, Maxine. Maxine was a Vargas Girl model and the Rose Bowl Queen in 1952, the year Frank was an All-American at the University of Southern California. They were California's golden couple on the exterior, but Maxine struggled with addiction even then . . . something that would escalate into a serious dependency that rocked Vicki's childhood and early adulthood, along with the lives of her older brothers, Jeff and Kyle.

When I became Frank's third wife in 1986, all three siblings were dealing with their own challenges as he grew into prominence on the national stage of sports and television. It took many years for Vicki and me to grow into the loving, trusting, warm, and tender relationship we share today. By the time Vicki had learned of her husband's many affairs, she and I had developed a beautiful friendship.

I'm so proud of the mature, loving woman Vicki has struggled long and hard to become.

KATHIE LEE: Obviously, you're my daughter via marriage to your dad. Tell me a little about the home life you grew up in.

VICKI: I remember living in eleven different places. I was born in Bakersfield. We drove a lot rather than flying. My mom was always trying to find places to stop that would be of interest or educational. We'd go way out of our way to see things, like Gettysburg. I saw a lot of the country when I was very young in a way that people don't anymore.

KATHIE LEE: You've always been a student. What were you taught as a child about God?

VICKI: I remember learning the Lord's Prayer and saying it every night. I also remember going to church when we lived in California. But when we moved to New York, I don't know if it was because Daddy was playing on Sundays, but we kind of fell out of the habit of going to church. Where I grew up, there were a lot of highly educated people, but no one was really talking about God. People went to church or synagogue on the weekends, but that was kind of it. I think I got my moral bearings more from my dad's idea of sportsmanship.

KATHIE LEE: You weren't an atheist, though, right?

VICKI: No. But I don't think we gave it a lot of thought. I do remember when people were sick, my mom would say a prayer. But there was no guidance on how to pray.

KATHIE LEE: Did you have any friends who were religious?

VICKI: I think as I got older I did. My husband, Michael, was religious, believe it or not. He needed to be forgiven every week, but he took the kids to church.

KATHIE LEE: Did you raise your kids as Catholics?

VICKI: No, especially not after he died. He'd take them to church, and I'd be in bed reading the *New York Times*!

KATHIE LEE: When I first met you, you were married to Michael.

VICKI: I was married in 1981. I would say the first twelve years were good years, before he went into this dark place. He went to rehab three times, and I would always go to the family programs. One of them was a religious place. Everyone focused on that addiction as a disease.

KATHIE LEE: What was his addiction?

VICKI: Alcohol and drugs. I know he always wanted to be better. When he died, we were talking again with a counselor. I didn't trust that he could kick all of his problems. When he stopped drinking, the womanizing got worse. He went and ran the marathon. Always extremes. And a lot of people who act out are addicted to the adrenaline rush that risk-taking behavior gives them. I think Michael was.

KATHIE LEE: He was seeing a priest, I remember, at the end?

VICKI: Yes, in Greenwich. He was trying to be better. We'll never know what happened.

KATHIE LEE: It was a shock to everyone how Michael had passed. You wanted to go to Israel, I know.

VICKI: I was thrilled to go. It was more about going to a historical place rather than the religious side. I learned so much. When I got there, I thought, "*I'll be with some great people: Cody, Cass, Christiana, Christine*"—people who knew *me*, so I felt safe. But I wasn't looking to have some kind of a revelation. And I don't think I really did. But what really stayed with me was the day we were at the Jordan River, getting baptized, and I was thinking, "*Am I a hypocrite?*" It's not like I had totally embraced everything. Then I thought, "*This is just a wonderful thing, watching people go in.*" And I said a prayer: "*Jesus, what should*

I say?" I was tired of being angry, and I wanted to forgive. And they dunked me in. I didn't fly down the river!

I remember thinking, "*That's the answer. I don't want to be angry.*" And I had a lot of anger toward a lot of people in my life. I don't know if I've learned to forgive, but I've let go of a lot of the anger. Sometimes I'll start ruminating, thinking about things that were bad, and I'll just say, "That's enough. It doesn't help. Forgive or let the anger go." I always feel better. It's harder some days than others.

KATHIE LEE: What comes to mind when you think about, or hear the name, Jesus?

VICKI: I guess I think now differently than I did before. I thought Jesus was a wise man and a teacher, like the Buddha or, you know, people who speak peace in the world. And now I really feel that He's the example of peace where everyone who speaks peace gets their inspiration from. So He's the standard where we learn the difference between right and wrong. I feel there's so much in this world that confuses people, and if you can find that standard of knowing what is the right and wrong thing to do, that is really important.

I think of Jesus as unconditional love, and I learned that He loves me, warts and all. He's here with us every moment. He doesn't put down rules, but He helps guide us to help ourselves. The more we know about Him, He did things that were unexpected, but they were the right things to do at that moment. And so He helps us find the rules within ourselves, and they're all based on the Golden Rule. How would you want to be treated? How you treat others is how you want to be treated. Every situation is different; what might be right in one situation may not work in another. That's why I say that He doesn't put down rules, but He helps us find in ourselves right and wrong.

When you say, "When you think about Jesus," I think about forgiving. He forgives me, and He forgives everybody. And it's really incredibly intimate when you know that. And I don't hold myself up as a big standard, but He gives me that ability to, I guess, let it go and think about what's really important, not me or my anger at things that have been done to me or things in my life.

KATHIE LEE: That's an intimacy you share with Him now that you didn't have before. The way you just talk to Him now. You said to me a long time ago, "I have faith envy."

VICKI: I do.

KATHIE LEE: It was almost like you were educated out of it. That's why I wanted you to go to Israel. To learn truth. The truth is what sets us free. I wanted you to go so that you would find truth, and when you found truth, that you would find peace. I remember you had something that happened on the shore on the side of the Jordan. The story I'm talking about is when you said, "I don't have enough faith," but it just has to be the size of a mustard seed.

VICKI: Oh yeah, and that was what it was for me. This little part of me that could accept. There's the big part of me that was like, "*This doesn't make sense.*" But you just do the best you can. That's all we're expected to do. And I really do think that finding out just that little bit of something extra in your life makes you so different. I don't think Jesus wants us to worship Him, but He embodies truth and love, and He wants us to find faith to believe that things are going to be okay.

KATHIE LEE: What were some of the other things that you wrote down?

VICKI: Just that I prayed that I would learn how to forgive more. I'm not there 100 percent, but I think that experience, especially at the Jordan River, and talking intimately with my new friends about my life when I was younger were His way, the Lord's way, of telling me that I needed to focus on Him. I need to stick with that, letting go of the anger and forgiving people. I don't think I've ever been a person who's not compassionate, but it's almost like a level above that, a compassion for our world and the compassion for myself that I do feel loved by God. And that's an unbelievable feeling. I wish I could have it all the time. When I do have it, it's like a calming thing, like a giant deep breath.

KATHIE LEE: The Word of God talks about how God collects our tears in a bottle. Every one is precious to Him.

VICKI: Yeah, but at a certain point, it's not about your history; it's about what you're going to do moving forward. And that's again one thing I feel appreciative learning about, the little I know about Jesus. One thing at a time for me, and for me that's forgiving people. You just have to walk away. It doesn't matter.

KATHIE LEE: I would say, just from my perspective, just the change in you that you feel that there is a person of God and that you are precious to Him, that you are loved, is the hugest change I've seen in you.

VICKI: I do think that everyone's important to the Lord. And He's created us to have free will so people will think of Him differently, but I'm grateful that the trip to Israel made me feel differently.

KATHIE LEE: Let's go back!

VICKI: Yeah!

CONCLUSION

WHO IS THE JESUS YOU KNOW?

EMILIE WIERDA

As we wrap our minds around these people and their unique stories, I'm hopeful you will see the diversity of the kingdom of heaven. Imagine with me for a minute what it will look like. We know God is there, and if we've trusted in Jesus as our Savior, we can know we will be there as well, but no doubt we'll be surprised by who else is behind those pearly gates!

I've often thought that if we'd take a moment to stand back from what we've seen before, the only view we've ever had, we'd realize that the kingdom of God is so much bigger than anything we could have ever dreamed. Much like a Google Earth view, we look at a map of our community and tend to focus on our experience and our neighbors, the ones we know. But when we zoom out to get a bigger picture, we realize there's so much more than what we'd imagined.

I believe that in heaven we will experience something like the apostle John must have experienced when he glimpsed the glory of heaven. He wrote in Revelation 7: "I looked, and there before me was *a great multitude that no one could count*, from every nation, tribe, people and language, standing before the throne and before the Lamb." Isn't that amazing? People from all walks of life, from all over the world, from all different journeys and encounters with Jesus—all praising God together.

So it's probably time now to come face-to-face with the all-important question: *Who is Jesus to you?*

As you think through your answer, consider this perspective from my friend and sister in the faith, Emilie Wierda. In 2012, Emilie and her husband, Craig, invited me to go to Israel with them. This trip changed my life because it introduced me to the rabbinical way of teaching. We spent time walking where Jesus walked, seeing and experiencing the people and culture of Israel, and learning who God is in ways that went beyond the words on a page to a new paradigm for thinking and believing.

KATHIE LEE: Emilie, tell us a little bit about the Jesus you know. Who is this Jesus that He should have the adoration of so many people on planet Earth?

EMILIE: Jesus is real. He has not evolved like some mythical god worshiped at some point in history. He lived at a specific time, in a specific place, among a specific people, to bring about a specific plan to heal a broken world. His purpose was and is to deliver humanity from the grasp of evil, sin, and death.

The fact that Jesus walked the face of the earth two thousand years ago is rarely disputed by any thinking person. The preponderance of evidence is so immense it withstands intellectual scrutiny at the highest levels. Time is marked and measured by His birth. Jesus is not just part of history. He is, in fact, the one who determined history. The apostle Paul's letter to the Colossians in the Bible says it this way: Christ "is before all things, and in him all things hold together."

KATHIE LEE: And Paul would know, right?

EMILIE: Oh yes, Paul would know. Before he encountered Jesus, Paul persecuted his fellow Jewish people who believed in Jesus. Yet, in His mercy,

Jesus came to heal Paul and make him holy. You can read the account in the book of the Acts of the Apostles, right in the Bible.

Paul's story reveals that Jesus will go to drastic measures to invite us into a love relationship! The God of the universe displayed His love, first to a man (Abraham), then to Abraham's family, then to a nation (Israel), and finally, through Jesus, to all the peoples of the world. Jesus humbled Himself to fit inside the womb of a Jewish woman and live the most difficult life of anyone at any time, just to demonstrate His love for us. Jesus made a way for *all* people from *all* nations of the earth to benefit from the same matrix for living—found in the inspired words of the Bible—and the same hope of eternal life previously promised only to His Jewish people.

KATHIE LEE: Yes, God's plan started with the Jews and is now for all nations! How did He accomplish this?

EMILIE: As Emmanuel, in the earth suit of Jesus, He lived and died to be the Redeemer and Savior of the world. More than two billion people today understand this and accept their gift of redemption. His kingdom continues to grow in places seen and unseen, every nation of the world.

KATHIE LEE: Amen! Why do you think Jesus' influence continues to flourish after two thousand years?

EMILIE: Because Jesus is the Healer, Counselor, and Friend. Consider some of the stories you heard from your friends and family. Consider the apostle Paul's story. Jesus heals, forgives, and restores real life to those who follow Him. And for those of us who receive His gift of forgiveness, Jesus sets us apart and makes us holy just as He is holy.

KATHIE LEE: I love the Hebrew word for "holy"—*kadosh*. It means we are "consecrated" and "set apart for sacred use."

EMILIE: Yes, Jesus makes His followers *holy*. This changes everything about the way we can look at life and our purpose for living. To be holy means we are profoundly loved, completely understood, and valued more highly than we can comprehend by our Creator. This is good news! While most of the world knows about Jesus, not everyone knows Him as friend and Savior.

KATHIE LEE: As we close this book, what is the most important thing you would like to say to the readers about Jesus?

EMILIE: I'd ask them, "What's your story about Jesus?"

The invitation is open. He says, "Come to me, all you who are weary and burdened." Might this be you today? He says to you, "Take my yoke [my example, my teachings, my way of living] upon you and learn from me."

You may be wondering, "*You want us to learn from You, Jesus? Not just know about You? Why?*" Jesus answers, "For I am gentle and humble in heart, and you will find rest for your souls. For my yoke is easy and my burden is light."

The God of gods and King of kings became love in human form to invite you and me to learn from Him how to really live—in wholeheartedness, without shame, in inexplicable joy. His Spirit is here, waiting to help us find *rest for our souls.*

I'm in. I hope you are as well! If not, consider this your invitation. I hope to meet you one day! Until then, know that you are loved beyond measure.

KATHIE LEE: That's beautiful, Emilie. Thank you so much for sharing.

My sincere hope and prayer is that my honest conversations with so many diverse people, who are in different places in their faith journeys and experiences with Christ, have left you with this thought: *Who is the Jesus I know?* If you and I could sit down in my cozy chairs and have an honest conversation about Jesus, what would you say? How were you first introduced to Jesus? Who has He been to you in your life so far? How do you experience Him today?

As you reflect on the Jesus you know, there is one last story I'd like to share with you, about a new friend, Alon, who recently moved near me. A reformed but observant Jew, he had a personal encounter with Jesus several years ago while grappling with an issue of self-forgiveness. Suddenly he sensed a presence with him, and he realized that it was Yeshua. Peace flooded his soul as Yeshua simply said to him, *"Alon, that's what I'm here for."* He immediately began to sob and sobbed for three days after. And he's been a completely changed man, with a completely changed heart ever since. That's the gospel in a nutshell, the good news of Jesus, the Messiah.

Friends, let's praise Him for bringing us to a deeper understanding of who Jesus is and what He is doing in the hearts and minds of people who are sometimes remarkably different from us!

I hope this begins a beautiful new movement of the Holy Spirit in your own heart and mind. But I also pray that we will all begin to show greater mercy toward our neighbors—the ones who look very much like us and, more importantly, the others who look nothing like us at all.

Shalom, y'all!

SCRIPTURES

INTRODUCTION: SURPRISING ENCOUNTERS WITH JESUS

- Jesus Christ is the same yesterday and today and forever. (Hebrews 13:8)
- Greater is he that is in you, than he that is in the world. (1 John 4:4 KJV)
- He who began a good work in you will carry it on to completion until the day of Christ Jesus. (Philippians 1:6)
- Jesus answered, "I am the way and the truth and the life. No one comes to the Father except through me." (John 14:6)
- You will seek me and find me when you seek me with all your heart. (Jeremiah 29:13)

1. A DIFFERENT KIND OF MISSIONARY: KRISTIN CHENOWETH

- The LORD God made a woman from the rib he had taken out of the man. (Genesis 2:22)
- God created mankind in his own image, in the image of God he created them. (Genesis 1:27)
- God demonstrates his own love for us in this: While we were still sinners, Christ died for us. (Romans 5:8)
- Ask and it will be given to you; seek and you will find; knock and

the door will be opened to you. For everyone who asks receives; the one who seeks finds; and to the one who knocks, the door will be opened. (Matthew 7:7–8)

- Christ died for our sins according to the Scriptures. (1 Corinthians 15:3)
- I want you to know that through Jesus the forgiveness of sins is proclaimed to you. Through him everyone who believes is set free from every sin. (Acts 13:38–39)
- [Jesus of Nazareth] is the one whom God appointed as judge of the living and the dead. (Acts 10:42)
- As I have loved you, so you must love one another. (John 13:34)
- Love your neighbor as yourself. (Matthew 22:39)
- Be still, and know that I am God. (Psalm 46:10)

2. FROM A JAIL CELL TO JOY: CYNTHIA GARRETT

- Do not conform to the pattern of this world, but be transformed by the renewing of your mind. (Romans 12:2)
- Put on the new self, which is being renewed in knowledge in the image of its Creator. (Colossians 3:10)
- I count all things but loss for the excellency of the knowledge of Christ Jesus my Lord. (Philippians 3:8 KJV)

3. FAITH AS A PART OF LIFE: KRIS JENNER

- "In everything, do to others what you would have them do to you." (Matthew 7:12)
- "When you give to the needy, do not announce it with trumpets, as the hypocrites do in the synagogues and on the streets, to be honored by others. . . . But when you give to the needy, do not let your left hand know what your right hand is doing, so that your giving may be in secret. Then your Father, who sees what is done in secret, will reward you." (Matthew 6:2–4)
- It would have been better for them not to have known the way of

righteousness, than to have known it and then to turn their backs on the sacred command that was passed on to them. (2 Peter 2:21)

- "For everyone to whom much is given, from him much will be required." (Luke 12:48 NKJV)

4. GROWING TOGETHER IN JESUS: JASON KENNEDY AND LAUREN SCRUGGS

- Pray without ceasing. (1 Thessalonians 5:17 NKJV)
- In Him we live and move and have our being. (Acts 17:28 NKJV)

5. DO NOT GROW WEARY IN WELL DOING: CHYNNA PHILLIPS BALDWIN

- "I will give them an undivided heart and put a new spirit in them; I will remove from them their heart of stone and give them a heart of flesh." (Ezekiel 11:19)
- If anyone is in Christ, the new creation has come: The old has gone, the new is here! (2 Corinthians 5:17)
- Because of his great love for us, God, who is rich in mercy, made us alive with Christ when we were dead in transgressions—it is by grace you have been saved. (Ephesians 2:4–5)
- We live by faith, not by sight. (2 Corinthians 5:7)
- "[The devil] is a liar and the father of lies." (John 8:44)
- If we confess our sins, he is faithful and just and will forgive us our sins and purify us from all unrighteousness. (1 John 1:9)
- Put on the full armor of God, so that you can take your stand against the devil's schemes. . . . In addition to all this, take up the shield of faith, with which you can extinguish all the flaming arrows of the evil one. (Ephesians 6:11, 16)
- Let us not be weary in well doing: for in due season we shall reap, if we faint not. (Galatians 6:9 KJV)

6. A DOUBLE PORTION OF SHAME, A DOUBLE PORTION OF BLESSING: ANNE FERRELL TATA

- Whatever is true, whatever is noble, whatever is right, whatever is pure, whatever is lovely, whatever is admirable—if anything is excellent or praiseworthy—think about such things. (Philippians 4:8)
- "With man this is impossible, but with God all things are possible." (Matthew 19:26)
- Where can I go from your Spirit? Where can I flee from your presence? If I go up to the heavens, you are there; if I make my bed in the depths, you are there. (Psalm 139:7–8)
- Wash away all my iniquity and cleanse me from my sin. . . . Then I will teach transgressors your ways, so that sinners will turn back to you. (Psalm 51:2, 13)
- Instead of your shame you will receive a double portion, and instead of disgrace you will rejoice in your inheritance. And so you will inherit a double portion in your land, and everlasting joy will be yours. (Isaiah 61:7)

7. JESUS AS A SOFT PLACE TO FALL: MEGYN KELLY

- We do not have a High Priest who cannot sympathize with our weaknesses, but was in all points tempted as we are, yet without sin. (Hebrews 4:15 NKJV)
- "He who is without sin among you, let him throw a stone at her first." (John 8:7 NKJV)

8. A MOTHER'S PRAYERS FOR JUSTIN BIEBER: PATTIE MALLETTE

- You intended to harm me, but God intended it for good. (Genesis 50:20)

- Because of the Lord's great love we are not consumed, for his compassions never fail. They are new every morning; great is your faithfulness. (Lamentations 3:22–23)
- It is God who works in you to will and to act in order to fulfill his good purpose. (Philippians 2:13)
- We all . . . are being transformed into his image with ever-increasing glory, which comes from the Lord, who is the Spirit. (2 Corinthians 3:18)
- Train up a child in the way he should go, and when he is old he will not depart from it. (Proverbs 22:6 NKJV)
- All your children will be taught by the Lord, and great will be their peace. (Isaiah 54:13)
- [God] is able to do immeasurably more than all we ask or imagine, according to his power that is at work within us. (Ephesians 3:20)
- "The thief comes only to steal and kill and destroy; I have come that they may have life, and have it to the full." (John 10:10)
- If we are faithless, he remains faithful, for he cannot disown himself. (2 Timothy 2:13)
- "My thoughts are not your thoughts, neither are your ways my ways," declares the Lord. "As the heavens are higher than the earth, so are my ways higher than your ways and my thoughts than your thoughts." (Isaiah 55:8–9)
- "I know the plans I have for you," declares the Lord, "plans to prosper you and not to harm you, plans to give you hope and a future." (Jeremiah 29:11)
- Whoever does not love does not know God, because God is love. (1 John 4:8)
- If the world hates you, keep in mind that it hated me first. (John 15:18)

9. CALLING JESUS ON THE MAIN LINE: JIMMIE ALLEN

- Encourage one another and build each other up. (1 Thessalonians 5:11)

- "Call to me and I will answer you and tell you great and unsearchable things you do not know." (Jeremiah 33:3)
- [Jesus] said to Thomas, "Put your finger here; see my hands. Reach out your hand and put it into my side. Stop doubting and believe." (John 20:27)
- The LORD upholds all who fall and lifts up all who are bowed down. (Psalm 145:14)
- Jesus Christ is the same yesterday and today and forever. (Hebrews 13:8)

10. A NEW PART OF THE FAMILY: GRANT GASTON

- If anyone is in Christ, the new creation has come: The old has gone, the new is here! (2 Corinthians 5:17)
- We know that all things work together for good to those who love God, to those who are the called according to His purpose. (Romans 8:28 NKJV)
- "Whoever believes in me, as Scripture has said, rivers of living water will flow from within them." (John 7:38)

11. YOU ARE NOT ALONE: CHUCK HARMONY AND CLAUDE KELLY (AKA LOUIS YORK)

- I can do all things through Christ who strengthens me. (Philippians 4:13 NKJV)
- To everything there is a season, a time for every purpose under heaven. (Ecclesiastes 3:1 NKJV)
- "What will it profit a man if he gains the whole world, and loses his own soul?" (Mark 8:36 NKJV)
- My heart says of you, "Seek his face!" Your face, LORD, I will seek. (Psalm 27:8)
- He was despised and rejected by mankind, a man of suffering, and familiar with pain. (Isaiah 53:3)

- "If anyone slaps you on the right cheek, turn to them the other cheek also. And if anyone wants to sue you and take your shirt, hand over your coat as well." (Matthew 5:39–40)
- "Greater love has no one than this: to lay down one's life for one's friends." (John 15:13)
- Jesus Christ is the same yesterday and today and forever. (Hebrews 13:8)

12. COURAGE WITH CONVICTIONS: JANICE DEAN

- The LORD is near to the brokenhearted and saves the crushed in spirit. (Psalm 34:18 ESV)

13. TAKING JESUS TO THE METAL MAINSTREAM: BRIAN WELCH

- He replied, "Whether he is a sinner or not, I don't know. One thing I do know. I was blind but now I see!" (John 9:25)
- "Woe to you, teachers of the law and Pharisees, you hypocrites! You are like whitewashed tombs, which look beautiful on the outside but on the inside are full of the bones of the dead and everything unclean." (Matthew 23:27)
- If anyone is in Christ, the new creation has come: The old has gone, the new is here! (2 Corinthians 5:17)

14. GOD LISTENS TO OUR PRAYERS: BRENDA SCHOENFELD

- God created mankind in his own image, in the image of God he created them. (Genesis 1:27)
- See what great love the Father has lavished on us, that we should be called children of God! (1 John 3:1)
- "Ask, and it shall be given you; seek, and ye shall find; knock, and it shall be opened unto you." (Matthew 7:7 KJV)

- Take delight in the LORD, and he will give you the desires of your heart. (Psalm 37:4)
- Our "God is a consuming fire." (Hebrews 12:29)
- No good thing does he withhold from those whose walk is blameless. (Psalm 84:11)
- Every good and perfect gift is from above, coming down from the Father of the heavenly lights, who does not change like shifting shadows. (James 1:17)

15. MESSENGER OF THE MESSIAH: RABBI JASON SOBEL

- We all, like sheep, have gone astray, each of us has turned to our own way; and the LORD has laid on him the iniquity of us all. (Isaiah 53:6)
- To provoke them to jealousy, salvation has come to the Gentiles. (Romans 11:11 NKJV)
- "Many are called, but few are chosen." (Matthew 22:14 NKJV)
- From the issuing of a decree to restore and rebuild Jerusalem, until Messiah the Prince, there will be seven weeks and sixty-two weeks. . . . Then after the sixty-two weeks, the Messiah will be cut off and have nothing. (Daniel 9:25–26 NASB)
- That I may know Him and the power of His resurrection, and the fellowship of His sufferings, being conformed to His death. (Philippians 3:10 NKJV)
- If anyone is in Christ, he is a new creation; old things have passed away; behold, all things have become new. (2 Corinthians 5:17 NKJV)

16. A SPIRITUAL FAMILY CONNECTION: DAVID, KELLY, AND NICHOLAS POMERANZ

- Before the mountains were born or you brought forth the whole world, from everlasting to everlasting you are God. (Psalm 90:2)

- "For everyone to whom much is given, from him much will be required." (Luke 12:48 NKJV)
- Therefore it is of faith that it might be according to grace, so that the promise might be sure to all the seed, not only to those who are of the law, but also to those who are of the faith of Abraham, who is the father of us all. (Romans 4:16 NKJV)
- He who began a good work in you will carry it on to completion until the day of Christ Jesus. (Philippians 1:6)

17. RESCUED BY LOVE: JIMMY WAYNE

- Religion that God our Father accepts as pure and faultless is this: to look after orphans and widows in their distress and to keep oneself from being polluted by the world. (James 1:27)

18. OUR COMMON GROUND IS SACRED GROUND: RAAKHEE MIRCHANDANI

- "Whoever believes in me, as Scripture has said, rivers of living water will flow from within them." (John 7:38)
- "In everything, do to others what you would have them do to you." (Matthew 7:12)
- "Love your neighbor as yourself." (Matthew 22:39)

19. A JOURNEY OUT OF ATHEISM: ROGER CHARLES

- "They shall destroy the walls of Tyre and break down her towers; I will also scrape her dust from her, and make her like the top of a rock. It shall be a place for spreading nets in the midst of the sea, for I have spoken," says the LORD God. (Ezekiel 26:4–5 NKJV)
- All Scripture is God-breathed and is useful for teaching, rebuking, correcting and training in righteousness. (2 Timothy 3:16)

- "In this world you will have trouble. But take heart! I have overcome the world." (John 16:33)

20. SOMETHING GREATER THAN OURSELVES: LISA KITTREDGE

- The word of God is alive and active. Sharper than any double-edged sword, it penetrates even to dividing soul and spirit, joints and marrow; it judges the thoughts and attitudes of the heart. (Hebrews 4:12)

21. THE RELUCTANT PROPHET: HUBIE SYNN

- There are different kinds of gifts, but the same Spirit distributes them. (1 Corinthians 12:4)
- To one there is given through the Spirit a message of wisdom, to another a message of knowledge by means of the same Spirit, to another faith by the same Spirit, to another gifts of healing by that one Spirit, to another miraculous powers, to another prophecy, to another distinguishing between spirits, to another speaking in different kinds of tongues, and to still another the interpretation of tongues. All these are the work of one and the same Spirit, and he distributes them to each one, just as he determines. (1 Corinthians 12:8–11)
- "Whoever believes in me will do the works I have been doing, and they will do even greater things than these, because I am going to the Father." (John 14:12)
- Jesus Christ is the same yesterday and today and forever. (Hebrews 13:8)

22. NOTHING IS IMPOSSIBLE WITH GOD: JOANNE MOODY

- Love the Lord your God with all your heart and with all your soul and with all your strength. (Deuteronomy 6:5)

- We know that in all things God works for the good of those who love him, who have been called according to his purpose. (Romans 8:28)
- The Spirit of the Sovereign Lord is on me . . . to bestow on them a crown of beauty instead of ashes. (Isaiah 61:1, 3)
- “Whoever believes in me will do the works I have been doing, and they will do even greater things than these, because I am going to the Father.” (John 14:12)
- “For with God nothing will be impossible.” (Luke 1:37 NKJV)
- [God] is able to do immeasurably more than all we ask or imagine, according to his power that is at work within us. (Ephesians 3:20)

23. FINDING THE JESUS WHO FORGIVES: VICKI GIFFORD KENNEDY

- “Then you will know the truth, and the truth will set you free.” (John 8:32)
- “If you have faith as small as a mustard seed, you can say to this mountain, ‘Move from here to there,’ and it will move. Nothing will be impossible for you.” (Matthew 17:20)
- Put my tears into Your bottle; are they not in Your book? (Psalm 56:8 NKJV)

CONCLUSION: WHO IS THE JESUS YOU KNOW?: EMILY WIERDA

- I looked, and there before me was *a great multitude that no one could count*, from every nation, tribe, people and language, standing before the throne and before the Lamb. (Revelation 7:9, emphasis added)
- He [Christ] is before all things, and in him all things hold together. (Colossians 1:17)
- If anyone is in Christ, he is a new creation; old things have passed away; behold, all things have become new. (2 Corinthians 5:17 NKJV)

- He who was seated on the throne said, "I am making everything new!" (Revelation 21:5)
- "Come to me, all you who are weary and burdened, and I will give you rest. Take my yoke upon you and learn from me, for I am gentle and humble in heart, and you will find rest for your souls. For my yoke is easy and my burden is light." (Matthew 11:28–30)

ACKNOWLEDGMENTS

My deepest thanks to all the individuals who worked so hard and helped me so much to bring this book to fruition.

To Albert Lee and Pilar Queen, my literary agents at UTA, who were so helpful in initially suggesting the concept.

And to Melissa Luther, my hairstylist, and Rebecca Halonso, my makeup artist, thank you once again for working your miracles.

To my good friends at HarperCollins: Matt Baugher, Debbie Wickwire, and Jennifer Stair, who enthusiastically and creatively helped me during the process.

And, of course, the ever-present angel in my life, Christine Gardner, who never ceases to amaze me with her faithfulness.

I'm deeply grateful to all, but all praise is reserved for my Messiah, Yeshua. My eternal thanks.

ABOUT THE AUTHOR

KATHIE LEE GIFFORD is the four-time Emmy Award–winning former cohost of the fourth hour of *Today*, alongside Hoda Kotb. After eleven years, Gifford stepped down from that role to pursue other creative endeavors.

Before *NBC News*, Gifford served as the cohost of *Live with Regis and Kathie Lee* for fifteen years. In 2015, Gifford was inducted into the Broadcasting & Cable Hall of Fame. In 2021, she received a star on the Hollywood Walk of Fame.

A playwright, producer, singer, songwriter, and actress, Gifford has starred in numerous television programs and movies in her forty-five-year career. She has written several musicals, including Broadway's *Scandalous*, which received a Tony nomination for Best Actress in 2012. Gifford also starred on Broadway in *Putting It Together* and *Annie*. In the fall of 2020, she released *Then Came You*, a film she wrote, produced, and starred in alongside Craig Ferguson. Gifford cowrote the score for the film with Brett James. In April 2019, she made her directorial debut with *The God Who Sees* oratorio, shot in Israel and based on a song she cowrote with Grammy-nominated Nicole C. Mullen.

Gifford has authored five *New York Times* bestselling books, *It's Never Too Late*; *The Rock, The Road, and the Rabbi*; *Just When I Thought I'd Dropped My Last Egg*; *I Can't Believe I Said That*; and the children's book *Party Animals*.

Gifford lends support to numerous children's organizations, including Childhelp, the International Justice Mission, and the Association to Benefit Children. She received an honorary degree from Marymount University for her humanitarian work in labor relations.

Connect with Gifford on Twitter and Instagram
@KathieLGifford